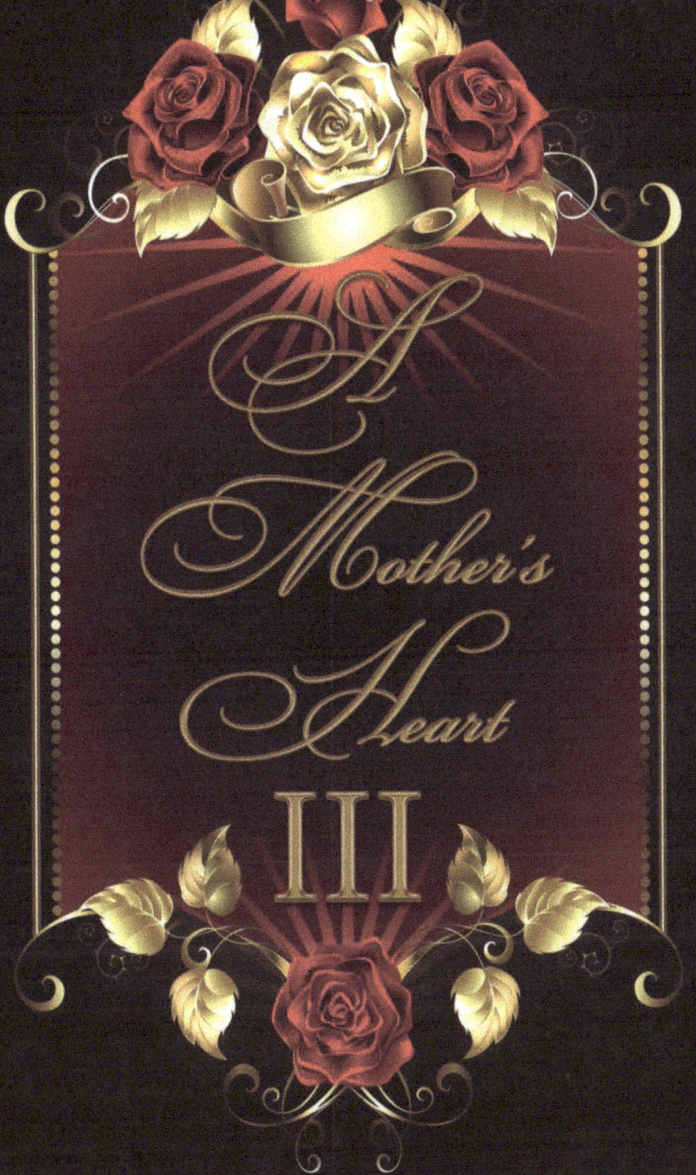

CLF Publishing, LLC.
9161 Sierra Ave, Ste. 203C
Fontana, CA 92335
www.clfpublishing.org

Copyright © 2017 by Cassundra White-Elliott. All rights reserved. No portion of this book may be reproduced, stored in a retrieval system, or transmitted by any form or any means electronically, photocopied, recorded, or any other except for brief quotations in printed reviews, without the prior permission of the publisher.

All rights reserved. No portion of this book may be reproduced, stored in a retrieval system, or transmitted by any form or any means electronically, photocopied, recorded, or any other except for brief quotations in printed reviews, without the prior permission of the publisher.

Cover Design by Senir Design. Contact information- info@senirdesign.com.

ISBN # 978-1-945102-16-5

Printed in the United States of America.

Dedications

This book is dedicated to mothers around the world who take time out of their own lives to nurture, teach, scold, and love the children they are blessed to have (whether they gave birth to them, adopted them, or if God blessed them spiritually with them). May God direct your paths as you interact with your children and may you be encouraged every step of the way.

Acknowledgements

I appreciate each of the twenty contributors to this book. Each chapter was written with love and respect for a wonderful woman. I thank each of you for your willingness to participate in this book and your adherence to all requests. This book is a success because of you!

Table of Contents

Introduction   7

How I Met My Mother by Yolanda Castro   11

Unbreakable Soul by Georgette Usi   15

Blessed All Your Life by Isaac Thompson   23

The Love of Two Sons by Nicholas and Justin Harrison   31

Love Never Lost by Ashleigh Morris   41

My Mother, God's Friend by Jerry G. Martin   51

Unconditional Love by Jourdan Jovel   59

An Irreplaceable Bond by Khalil Flemister   63

Forgiveness by Audrey Albrecht   71

The Strength of One Woman by Cathy Vines-Nichols   77

Mommy and Me by Akayla Clayton   83

Through it All, I'm Still Standing by Dalejuan Jackson   89

Mommy by Quantanique Williams   97

The Love I Have for My Mother by Millicent Redd   101

A Mother Like None Other by Ayleeyah Nichols   107

Mom- Gentle Strength by Julia Lary   117

A Mother of Strength and Love by Maria Guzman   125

A Life of Inspiration Tyler Kowalski-Foley & Haley Keil   129

A Caring Soul Fernando Lescano   137

A Letter to My Mother by Elaine M. Tolentino   149

My Best Friend by Karen Ruiz   155

The Gift of Salvation for Non-Believers   159

About the Editor   165

Introduction

Mothers around the world have dedicated their lives to their children. They take seriously the task of nurturing, loving, developing, educating, and preparing them for life. However, unbeknownst to most mothers, they face a task that is embedded with many challenges, such as the life of a teenager, rebellion, the terrible two's, etc. Despite the challenges, mothers forge ahead with the task at hand. With the love they have for their children, they endure many hardships, even when the same love is not returned or fully appreciated. They strive to stay focused on the task at hand and refrain from allowing anything to deter them.

On this road of motherhood, women embark upon this journey without a manual. They enter motherhood not fully knowing what to expect from the children they will raise. They don't know what the children's behavior patterns will be, their likes or dislikes, or how they will respond to different life experiences. Motherhood is truly on-the-job training.

Through the joys and pains, through the tears and metaphorical rain, mothers press on. At times, their love is equally reciprocated while at other times it is not. At times, children are found to be treasures, and at other times, they are not. At times, children are found to be obedient, while at other times, they are not. One constant you will find is – regardless of how the children are, mothers would not trade their children in for anything else in the world. Mothers take their children as they are!

Because of this unconditional love, their endurance, and their commitment, mothers are worth their just due. They are worthy of praise, and they are worthy of honor.

In this book, you will read the stories of many mothers written by their children who wanted to honor them. Some of the mothers have passed on, but their memories remain. The other mothers who are being honored are alive and well. They will have the opportunity to read the words their children have written.

Please note- this book is not to paint mothers as saints. It is to show their humanness, their successes and their mistakes, their triumphs and their trials. It is to honor them for all they have done. By no means are mothers perfect, but with their love, they have seen their children through many battles. It is because of who they are/were that we are who we are.

After examining the lives of my grandmother, mother and aunts and being a mother and grandmother myself, I know the sacrifices a mother makes for her children. A mother always wants what is best for her children. She will give them the dress from her back and the food from her plate to make sure her children are well cared for.

As you read through the story of each mother, I want you to think about a mother you know. She may be your mother, your grandmother, your aunt, a friend, a cousin, a sister, a mother-in-law, or a co-worker. As you think about this mother, think about how you can encourage her. Whether you know it or not, mothers need to be encouraged. They need to know that their labor is not in vain.

When my mother was alive, I told her, "Thank you for loving me. Thank you for teaching me. Thank you for placing me above all else. Thank you for being my mother."

Today, I encourage the young mothers in my life. I tell them when they are doing a great job with their children, especially the mother of my grandchildren. Also, I give them pointers (in love) when they can do better. I believe my words encourage them to be tender, loving mothers. As I speak to the young mothers, I must remember that they are relatively new to mothering, and they are learning through the joys and challenges of motherhood, just as I did when raising my two sons.

To all mothers- we cannot change the past. We cannot undo any mistakes we may have made. All we can do is strive for a better tomorrow for ourselves and for our children. Be encouraged! You are not alone in this job of motherhood. There are many mothers who share your concerns, your worries, and your fears.

Motherhood is a joy. Enjoy every moment of your adventure and spend as much time with your children that you can. Love them with all heart, and whether you experience ups and downs or a smooth ride, your children will never forget your love.

Dr. Cassundra White-Elliott

A Mother's Heart

How I Met My Mother

by
Yolanda Castro

A Mother's Heart

My mother is a wonderful mother. I love her to death. She taught me my values, my principles, and made me the person I am today. She always encouraged me to better myself, to be a productive woman, and to never depend on anyone to be successful. I received so much from her in a short period of time. I met her when I was a year old and was under her care for seven years. You might ask me, "How is this possible?" Well, my mother is my grandmother. She taught me to be humble, to be compassionate, and to be considerate of other people. She told me you cannot judge a person by what he/she has. You cannot judge a person by his/her income or what type of house he/she has. You must judge the heart. The many lessons she taught me have helped me make decisions in my life.

I thank her for everything she did for me. I understand the way I was introduced into her life was unusual, but she accepted me regardless. My grandmother took care of my needs with very little help from anyone. She was my mother and father at the same time she was raising her own children.

My best memories come from my childhood experiences. Climbing on a tree and singing to the clouds to allow rain to come were wonderful experiences. I can still smell the wet dirt after the rain had fallen. My grandmother taught me those songs and more. She made corn dolls for me from cornstalks, and those were fun to play with. Also, she made rag dolls for me to play with, and she made clothes for them. One of the things I learned from her was how to knit and how to crochet. I treasured her so much, and I would not exchange my childhood for anything else.

About the Author

Yolanda Castro is a single mother of four who was raised in Michoacan, MX by her grandparents Maria and Alfonso. She was born in Indio, CA. She has been an active parent volunteer for ten years in Coachella District. She is currently attending college and sitting as a Board Member in the Coachella Valley Unified School District.

Unbreakable Soul

by
Georgette Usi

This is for you, Mom.
Thank you for inspiring me to keep staying strong in life.

My mom is the strongest woman I've ever known. There are a million of reasons why. I am proud and blessed that I'm her daughter, and I will forever be glad. First, allow me to introduce who my mom is. My mother's name is Mary Jean. She was born in a province in the Philippines, as well as my grandma and my mother's six siblings. They never lived a wealthy life. So, my mom had to work at a young age to help her mother and her siblings. She is the sixth of her siblings, is family oriented, and is a hard-working person. She always helps her mom and siblings in every possible way. She is average height and weight, with brown skin, black eyes and black short hair. She enjoys dancing and is a very friendly person, to the point where she knows everyone in the neighborhood.

Due to the lack of money, she didn't get a chance to enroll in a college or university. After graduating high school with high honors, she applied for a job in a sewing factory. She also worked in a fast-food chain as a waitress, which is where she met my dad. My mom and my dad met when my mom was nineteen years old, while my dad was twenty-six years old. My mom got pregnant in an early age, and my mom and my dad had their first baby when my mom was twenty. Even though my mom was very young, once that happened she understood the responsibilities and duties she would then have to undertake.

From being a young lady who was living her life with nothing to worry about, she turned into a mature woman ready to be a loving mother and raise a beautiful child, a daughter. Five years later, they had a son. My mom and my dad unfortunately broke up three years after I was born; I was their third child. With my father gone, I was raised by my mom with the help of my grandma. My mom told me I was never planned. She told me that she and my father only expected and planned to have two kids. But she told me, although I was never planned, she was thankful to God because of me. She said I was both a surprise and a gift from above. Growing up, I lived in a village in the city of Manila with my mom, my sister, and my brother. My mom took care of all three of us.

There are many memories of how my mom showed her love for us, her children. My mom is my first and greatest teacher. She taught me how to write and read when I was five years old. That is the reason why I was able to get into first grade without taking any preschool classes. As I grew older and older, she continued to teach me how to be a loving and better person by teaching me good values. I remember when I was six years old as a first grader. My classmates bullied me, and I went home crying, telling my mom that I didn't ever want to go to school again because of those girls who bullied me.

The next day, she went with me to school and talked to those girls who bullied me. After that, those two girls approached me after class and told me they were sorry, and we became friends. My mom is my protector. My mom is humble, but at the same time, she knows when to fight for what is right. My mom taught me to be a good person. She always tells me to stay humble. She is the most humble person I've ever known. She's always down to earth with people even if they are trying to bring her down. She always does her best and shows them her true kind self.

But what's amazing about her is that she is so protective over her loved ones that she'll do anything no matter what it takes to ensure their safety and happiness. Furthermore, my mom is my doctor. Every time I am sick, she always takes care of me. She'll always ask me what I want for breakfast, lunch, and dinner. She always makes me macaroni soup every time I am sick, and it always makes me feel better. She never leaves me; she rubs my head and pats my back until I fall asleep.

When I was in high school as a freshman, my mom was the one who woke me up to go to school. And, my breakfast would be ready as soon as I awoke. Usually, she made me a buttered toasted sandwich, which is my favorite breakfast. She would not let me go to school if I didn't eat breakfast. She said I would not have energy and mental alertness in class if I didn't eat because breakfast is the most important meal of the day. My mom is a good cook; one of my favorite dishes of hers is her Filipino spaghetti. I think it's the most delicious spaghetti I've ever tasted and will ever taste. It is honestly better than Italian restaurants like Olive Garden.

Another memory I have is when my sister got pregnant at the age of twenty-five. She kept her situation secret because she was scared to tell the family because our family knew nothing about her boyfriend, plus my sister was in a state where she was not capable and not ready to start a family. Months passed, and my sister felt it was the right time to tell my mom about her pregnancy. So, when my sister finally surrendered to my mom, telling her that she was sorry and that she was pregnant, my mom's first reaction was a mother's instinct. She cried, and instead of getting mad at my sister for keeping the secret for so long, she was worried about my sister and her baby's health. In that moment, I saw how a mother's heart is, that whatever happens, even if her child had gone wrong, she'll love and care for her children unconditionally.

My mom is diligent and hard working. At home, she does all the housework even when she doesn't need too. She cleans everything. She never gets tired of doing house chores. She's such a supermom. She taught me house chores as well. She taught me how to clean dishes and how to properly wash clothes by hand. She never spoiled us. Instead, she taught us things we needed to know for us to grow. So, at home, we all do our own dishes and our own laundry, which I think is necessary in terms of raising children because nowadays, a lot of children don't know how to do those things.

On another note, as I was growing up, I saw how my mother was broken from the relationship she had with my dad. She loved my dad so much that she cried every night thinking about what was wrong. It broke my heart every time I saw her cry. She told me everything about them. She told me how they met, how my dad pursued her, how they fell in love with each other, how they had their children, and how my dad left her, left us. She also showed me all the letters my dad gave to her while they were still together. The letters are extremely romantic and full of love. That made me question what had happened to them. How could two people who are madly in love with each other end up breaking each other's heart?

You never know how tricky love is; it's a game that involves risk. You let someone come into your life, not knowing if that person will bring joy or tears. My mom became our mother and father, while at the same time showing me how strong and independent a woman she is. Seeing that, I said to myself that I would make my mom happy and proud by graduating college and being able to help her, as she helped me. I will forever look up to my mom as my hero and my motivation for staying strong in life during rough times.

About the Author

Georgette Jean Usi is an eighteen-year-old college student at Cypress College and Fullerton College while working full time as a shift leader in a restaurant. Her goal is to graduate with an Associates of Science Degree of Flight Attendant, be able to work for an airline, have a chance to travel the world, and learn different cultures. She was born in Manila, Philippines and moved to California, Los Angeles when she was sixteen years old. When she was in middle school, she was not interested in the idea of reading books. She graduated high school at La Mirada High School in California with honors where she took language arts class and had the chance to read one of the most brilliant novels of F. Scott Fitzgerald: "The Great Gatsby." This led her to open her eyes to writers' astonishing talent and imagination. Her favorite genre to read is romantic novels. Three of her most favorite books are "Beautiful Disaster" by Jamie McGuire, "Me Before You" by Jojo Moyes, and "My Name is Memory" by Ann Brashares.

A Mother's Heart

Dr. Cassundra White-Elliott

Blessed All Your Life

The Stella Thompson Story
by
Isaac Thompson

Stella and Isaac

A Mother's Heart

One's appreciation of long life and the numbering of your days by God takes on a special aura when memories are encased in love. Maybe it's because I reside in a place where movies are made, that early recollections cast Mom as the first glamorous vision of my mind's eye. In those long ago days, there were restaurants with long counters for those whose preference was counter service. So when I saw Mother at work behind the counter in a uniform, all put-together to deal with the public, so stylish that repeat customers were a certainty, the vision was like those women on television. As a tiny kid, I remember the smile that made me feel special and the beverage she gave me in that restaurant-type tall thick glass. Since she too was young, her figure was thin and curvy, just like the actresses on T.V.

The past few decades gave rise to the term latch-key kids. I guess as a society, we're prone to developing terms descriptive of an individual or a family's composition or circumstances. For minorities, it seems that households with two working parents have been the norm since seemingly forever.

It had been the time of year when fall was giving way to winter, and I found myself sitting on the stoop of our Long Island home, waiting for Dad, when dropping temperatures led to a decision (perhaps resulting in automatic discipline) from some inner place.

I decided it was too cold to merely wait, so going to the rear of our home, I broke a small basement window, because well, I was cold. The results were anything but unpleasant; rather, the next day, Mom gave me my own house key! Being all of seven years old, I realized Mother believed in me as a person. Of course, the responsibility came with a list of do's and a "don't lose it" (and a requisite safety pin "so I wouldn't lose it"). Raising responsible children requires trust, a belief that the parents' words will be heeded, and they were.

A life-long aspect of character grew from the latch-key norm of those times. That element was a work ethic, established as the norm, from the earliest memory of Mom and Dad, but an unspoken life example delivered simply by observation. Even without the privileges I've enjoyed, due to higher education benefits, Mom always found a way to earn more, keeping up with established professional positions. The restaurant work gave way to nursing and licensed health care, establishing an equal footing in the mother/father dynamic.

Comfortable living and upwardly mobile households bring expectations. For Mom's three boys, it meant doing well in school; after all, we had no excuses. When love is combined with good-provision, it's up to the children to make their parents proud. Since Dad was former military, he was not given to heaping praise; it was simply his way to expect one to do as expected.

So it was Mother, the one that would occasionally praise, who would cause my chest to proudly swell. Then, came the lesson; comportment, behavior carried as much weight as doing one's best in any subject. I can only recall it as pre-high school and the dreaded report card day. Well, there I was head high and confident. Good grades, yeah, with one glaring exception: the red-letter in citizenship. Having become socially self-assured, I'd been too talkative. When the evening of reckoning arrived, all the other grades didn't matter. I'd blown it by talking too much! Stern words left me feeling small, level with the carpet, unable even to offset the single issue by pointing out academic achievement. A lifelong lesson was never lost. Sure, Dad was Dad, but when your mother is not happy, the whole house feels it. Thank God! When you're raised with standards originating from God-Almighty, well, it establishes an expectancy of being all you can be- period. Character and behavior, I later learned, had been ingrained by my mom's dad, and no son of hers would be exempt from carrying the mantle of God-fearing, God-obeying, Christian folk. Uh, I think the lesson took!!!

As often happens, love is extended from mother to son in ways neither could foresee as being life shaping. An otherwise normal Saturday morning has become a lifelong blessing. Strange, how the memory of a day five decades ago remains so vivid. Mom instructed this middle son in the basics of cooking. It was not just the cooking; the fare was common-place food: bacon, grits and eggs. What was not common was wisdom's foresight, her realizing that no matter the twists and turns of life, a man should be able to take care of himself in all aspects. In light of that awareness, not only was I schooled in self-preservation, but also in things from food to healthy living, housekeeping and other things too numerous to recall that provided life lessons designed for self-sufficiency.

We don't always realize at the time, but our care and instruction for one child has generational reverberations. During my times as a single dad, occasionally my job would require travel. The proximity of my parent's home meant minimal disruption for my son, although at the time that provided small comfort in easing the guilt of being away from home. It was not until years later that I learned my folks were somewhat put off by the in-depth instructions I would leave. You see the guilt was two-fold, not wanting to impose on Mom whose job had been done was the second aspect. But with written instructions, lunch menus, pre-ironed clothes and on and on, I did not take into account, they'd **raised me**! So what took place and is still resounding generationally is love, abiding in all things. Having seen it looking back, witnessing it in the here and now, and reveling in what's to come, leaves a son with an all too insufficient "Thanks, Mom."

Life's journey, the one we share, carries some pain and losses (husband-dad, son-brother and so forth) and is, as with life itself, peppered with highs and lows. A low water mark came on Father's Day 1993, when settling in and basking in the one day a good dad can feel good through the outpouring of love in its purest that darn phone rang. The message was inconceivable. Mom's life was jeopardized by a car accident while traveling. So horrible was the thought that I hoped it was a cruel prank. It was not.

While details are too numerous and varied, my mother emerged from a near comatose state three days later and subsequently was stabilized enough for us to return and have her surgery, involving metal-plates, screws, etc., overseen by our family doctor. The depth of despair I cannot fully convey, but it was my first intense petition to the Rock, our Savior Jesus, to spare my mother; and the only time I ever uttered "take me instead," reasoning that my son has for himself a mom second to none. Interspersed during the time of waiting for Mom's vital signs to be restored were days spent alone in Bakersfield motel room, fielding phone calls at all hours, from Hawaii to Florida. Over and over, I'd hear, "Well, I'm glad you're with her," which really made me want to scream!

When one feels helpless and despair takes him somewhere he has never been, only our Lord can gird His own to do what they're called to do. That accident changed my mother's life, requiring special consideration at x-ray machines, etc., but it also changed my life, as I still have a most difficult time dealing with Father's Day of '93.

"How do you thank the one," is a portion of the songwriter's words for those whose caretaking is beyond description. Well, perhaps, believers can grasp that of all else, **a legacy of faith**, of being a **people of God** is the single most important thing we give to those whose lives our Father entrusted to our care. When it comes to my mom, I know God loves me by whom and through whom He gave me life. Since our human journey carries necessary struggles, designed for our eternal well-being, no matter, come what may, this mother's son can always recall her singular declarative view of her second born: "You've been blessed all your life." Yes Mother, I have, and it all began with you.

Praise be to God!

A Mother's Heart

Dr. Cassundra White-Elliott

The Love of Two Sons for Their Mother

The Shonda Evans-Harrison Story
by
Nicholas and Justin Harrison

The Harrison Family: Shonda, Justin, Nicholas, and August

A Mother's Heart

Nicholas' Testimony

Someone to shelter and guide us, to love us, whatever we do, with a warm understanding and infinite patience, to watch over her children and treasure them all through the years, a mother, that is.

My existence has been momentously influenced by my mother, Shonda Evans-Harrison. Responsive, nurturing, genuine, and protective would best describe my mother's merits. She is one of the few individuals who have aided me through hectic circumstances. She is my go-to person. If something happened to me or if I needed someone to talk to, she would be the first I turn to. And though I turn to her often and constantly with some form of request, she never turns me away. She was able to answer every question I had, to the best of her knowledge. The majority of the times we communicated, I did not comprehend what she meant, and she recognized my confusion.

I believe admiration is a form of respect. I admire my mother just as much as she admires me. I admire how fair-minded she is. She does not favor anyone over another. She treats people evenly.

Because I am the eldest, I was taught that I will be held responsible for my brother and the rest of the family if something happens to my parents. I admit I was afraid once she told this to me. But, I knew exactly what she meant during the process of growing up. My understanding of my mother's viewpoint helped me become a healthier, responsible individual. She had also taught me to be myself and have positive people surround me. She convinced me to believe that being different was something special to be proud of. Being yourself leads to a better lifestyle. This is how I became well-rounded and social. My mother knows what is best for me and my brother. She motivates us to be prepared to make the right choices.

I knew when something bothered her, and I understood when it was necessary to give her space, but I also knew how to comfort her when no one was available. The relationship between my mother and me is indefinable. We were able to help each other, which was odd for me to realize that I could be there for someone who is always supportive.

I have witnessed the traumatic times my mother had struggled to further her education, raise a family, and find employment. As independent as she was, her actions and choices always resulted in an optimistic outcome. There was something about her that I yearned for. I grew up thinking she had superpowers to make her solve problems efficiently. The reason for this was because she was also raised that way by her parents.

Ever since my maternal grandmother passed away, the qualities I saw in my mother dropped. It was a dreadful period. My mother became weak and hopeless for a long time. This frightened me so much that I did not know what to do. Days were spent in her room, reminiscing about her life through old photographs and letters. This was an unforgettable experience that helped me shape my outlook on life.

My mother was living in silence and was complex about her situations. Because I was scared at first, my mind changed from fearing her to sympathizing with her. I realized from her eyes, she had a durable resistance to illness and a strong will to live an ordinary life under such terrible circumstances. Giving my small gifts, I also received from her a more valuable gift- true happiness. True happiness comes from the simple things in life and from trying to make others happy. The more of it we give to others, the more we will have for ourselves.

What I love most about my mother is how she is capable of making things and life easy when it isn't. A while before I came into existence, my mother had become saved. She taught my brother and me about the Lord. She kept the Bible as a guide to raising us. In turn, we all got saved, and the Lord has continued to be the guide in our lives even when we were not around her.

My mother has proven that the qualities of determination and perseverance are both essential to have in order to undertake our mindsets. She has lectured my brother and me on the fundamental values of life necessary to survive in this world. By doing so, we have extensive conversations about her experiences, memories and accomplishments. I look forward to utilize my mother's attributes for future situations.

My mother is actually an ordinary woman, but in her tiny appearance lays an extraordinary fortitude, perseverance, an altruistic soul, and a very kind heart. The kind of mother who brought me up with her whole kindly heart, the kind of persistent woman with strong willpower who had to face the toughest challenges in life, and the kind of person who always demonstrated great eagerness for every tragic lives without requiring anything in return and great willingness to help everyone's misery though she did not have much. My mother taught me more than anyone else, not only inspired in me the strength to overcome hardships in my life, but also left me with invaluable life lessons. Her fortitude and perseverance, as well as her kind heart, have encouraged me to grow up to live the life of an authentic person, a life engulfed with perseverance and determination, a life with heartfelt eagerness to love and to receive love from every one and optimistic beliefs in the future.

I am highly thankful of the awareness to appreciate our mothers on a designated day. Nevertheless, mothers ought to receive the praise they deserve for all of their hard work and effort. Because I am a child by heart, regardless of age, I will continue to call her "mommy." It does not bother her whenever I say this. She mentions that I will always be her baby no matter how old I am. I love her so much, and I appreciate everything she has done.

Suffering through her absence for a number of years (due to her hospitalization), my family and I are able to continue functioning the way my mother would want us to. She always told me that I should be alright and know what to do if she is not here. This is a challenge I am prepared to face. It has been a fearsome roller coaster. Lamentably, numerous events took place without her support. Birthdays, school events, and family get-togethers have not been the same without her. I miss her dearly. I feel miserable hearing other people bring up their mothers and how much fun they have with them.

I look to her in hopes that someday I will be as content, as resilient, and as coherent as she. She has taught me the most important thing in life- never give up on yourself. I thank her dearly for aiding me to become who I am today. I would have never made it as far as I have without her comfort. The precious lessons from my mother are the luggage for me to go on my road and discover new horizons of knowledge and make my dream become a reality instead of just a dream. I owe my strength to my mother. Her life experience has made me more vigorous to face every hardship, to overcome each failure, and move on. Far more meaningfully, I also realize the invaluable gift of life and true happiness to view the world more optimistically and to believe in a brighter future.

Justin's Testimony

My mother has been an inspiration to me since the day I was born. I learned to love my mom since we first met, and I will always love her. She always protects me and supports me through thick and thin. Whenever I am happy or whenever I am sad, my mother is with me. She helps me with hard problems in life and is glad for some of the choices I've made.

From raising me to teaching me life lessons, my mother has always been there for me from the start. My mother has raised me to be a great man in life. The way I act is no differently than the way any other person should. I was raised with respect, manners, my own dignity, and to have my own self confidence. Every day, I see kids and how they act around each other. Then, I think to myself, *I'm glad I was raised properly by a mother who cares.*

One of the lessons my mother taught me was to treat everyone I know with respect. She has treated me with respect, the majority of the time, to help me learn. I had even asked her, "What if I treat someone with respect, but he doesn't choose to respect me the same way?" That's when she told me it does not matter if people treat me terribly. As long as I know how to treat people properly, with the right amount of respect, I will have respect for myself.

Ever since I learned that from her, I have treated most people with respect. And I honestly do not care what others say or think about me. I have also learned from my mother that I can succeed at anything I work hard at. She always wants me to succeed in school, so I can have a good education and go to college when I get older. She also wants me to succeed in following my dream of becoming a doctor. I have wanted to become a doctor because of my mom. I learned all about doctors and how to become one from her.

I love how my mother and I look alike. In similarities, we have the same eyes, nose, smile, and most importantly, the same personality. I would always say what my mother would say, eat what my mother would eat, and also act the same way she did. She always called me her little twin. And her friends and our family would call me "Little Shonda." Hearing that from others would always make me smile, and it would make me happy inside.

What I didn't understand about my mother is that she sometimes kept her feelings inside. I had even told her that it's not healthy to ball up all of your feelings and not tell anyone about it. I was afraid that my mother would become insanely stressed with everything around her. If something terrible had happened, or if she were to be upset, she would just hold all of her feelings inside, until she would be able to let it out. If my mother was going through a hard time with work or family, she would take her anger out on my brother, my father, and me. But I understood what she was going through.

Sometimes I felt that if I bothered my mom while she was upset, I would get yelled at and make her even more upset than she already was. Little did I know that every now and then, my mother actually needed for me to come bother her and talk to her. Every day when my mom would come home from work, I would ask her, "How was your day, Mom?" She would then smile and tell me how her day went. Even if she was stressed, me asking her that question would please her.

My mother would always sit down with me and tell me why she was upset and what her problems were. After our little talks, she would thank me for taking the time to sit and listen to her and help her solve her problems. Seeing my mother happy made me happy. I knew that when she was happy, nothing would ever change.

Whenever my mom would be in a good mood, she would always call me her "Jiglet." She started calling me that when I was born; I never knew what that meant and was never told how she came up with that word. But it didn't matter, because my mother loved calling me that name, and she loved me as well. Knowing that my mother loved me meant everything to me. I love my mom with all my heart. And she had once told me, "Whenever I yell or scream at you, I'm simply doing that because I love you."

From there on, I never really cared if my mother would yell at me or get upset with me. Because I knew that she loved me no matter what. The one thing that I admire about my mother is how she always cares about others. She is kind, incredibly friendly, loving, and so warm hearted. Not only would she care, but she would take care of the ones she loved. From taking care of me and my brother, to taking care of other family members, my mother was there for everyone. She would try her best to please everyone.

My mother is an independent, strong, smart, confident woman. I am grateful to have a mom that takes care of me. I know that I can always rely on my mother for help, advice, and all sorts of lessons she can teach me. When I struggle to bring myself to happiness, my mother is there to help me. Never have I taken anything that my mother has done for me for granted. My mother cooks for me, cleans for me, buys me clothes, she keeps a house over my head, and keeps me safe.

I believe that my mother, Shonda Evans-Harrison, is the greatest mother that myself or anyone else can have. She gave birth to me and my older brother Nicholas. I'm proud to be called her son. I would not be able to enjoy the rest of my life without my mother in it. I am who I am today because of my wonderful mother. I would not be here today if it weren't for my mother.

I honestly care about my mom, and I wouldn't want anything unfortunate to happen to her. She is everything I could ever ask for in a mother. The most important thing I love about my mother is that no matter how many times we fight, no matter how many times we argue, even if I am not the best child she could ever have, she always makes me feel that I am the best gift she ever received from God.

Looking back at the wonderful times I had with my mother, I remember she is the most positive and important influence in my life. She is a diligent and determined woman who has left me with the right direction in life. But more importantly, she has helped me appreciate this life she has given me with happiness.

Dr. Cassundra White-Elliott

Love Never Lost

The Cressie Latrice Daniels-Marshall Story
by
Ashleigh Morris

Cressie and daughters: Ashleigh and Kyleigh

A Mother's Heart

It wasn't always perfect, nor was it always bad. We all have a time in our lives where things just don't go our way or how we had imagined they would.

Growing up, I had a great life. I didn't want for anything. I got everything I wanted and more, and my life couldn't be any better. No, I didn't grow up with both parents in the home, but I had both parents in my life. I was my mother's only child up until three months before my seventh birthday. I didn't want a sister or a brother, but I had no choice in that.

The following year in August of 1998, I experienced my first heart break. I lost my grandmother to cervical cancer at the age of 47 years old. I was only seven, so I didn't know what my mom was going through, nor did I give it much thought. Life went on, and I still had a great life even having a little sister. We took mini family trips, and we were always together with my uncle's family.

Fast forwarding to about 2002, my mom had the gastric bypass surgery, and I believe that's when everything changed. Once she lost the weight, she started going out and being around different crowds of people.

In 2005, I began to notice her constant drinking. I'm not sure how long it had been going on, but that is when I opened my eyes. That same year, I moved with my dad for my sophomore year of high school, only to move back with my mom the following year as I had to be a protector for my sister, who had seen and been around too much for my liking. People are different when they are drunk.

Unfortunately for me, my mother was not the happy type of drunk. She would get drunk and angry, and she would become a person whom I did not know. People would call her by the name Mello, and I feel that was an alter ego. To this day, I can't stand for a person to call her Mello. The mother I knew and loved was Cressie. This Mello person that she turned into when she drank, I often felt, did not love me. I expressed how I felt to my mom a few times once she was sober, and she would apologize and let me know how much she does in fact love me.

There was a program in my apartment building, and they would set the kids up on summer jobs for three weeks, and they would get paid $300 at the end of the three weeks. I was planning to go shopping at the outlets, so I gave my money to my mom to hold until I was going. The day before I was set to go, I got in trouble for something, but she still let me go. However, she told me she would not be giving me my money that I had worked for. Imagine that!

Summer 2007 was when my life hit rock bottom. Don't get me wrong. I was a child that got whippings and punishments. So even though I had a good life, if I did the crime, I paid the time. It seems though the older I became, the harsher she became, even when I hadn't done anything to deserve it.

When I was sixteen, I was going to summer school and working my first job at Knott's Berry Farm. My school was on the same street as my job, so I didn't mind catching the bus, but when I got off at midnight, my ride should have been there. Right? Wrong!!

There were a few times I had to wake people up out of their sleep to come and pick me up because my mom was out at the club and forgot she was supposed to pick me up from work. How she managed to forget about her sixteen year old getting off work at 12am is beyond me, but hey what could I do?

The day I will never forget is December 22, 2007. My hardheaded sister and I were 'play' fighting. I told her over and over again to stop because I did not want to play around with her anymore. I was not supposed to hit my sister, but I had continually told her to leave me alone. When I did hit her, it sounded louder than it really was and she became dramatic.

My mom started yelling at me and told me, "You're almost 300 pounds. You shouldn't be hitting on her."

By that time, I was in my room, so in my defense I yelled out to her, "I'm not close to 300 pounds!" She ran into my room, and she called me every name in the book. By that time, I was called a b**** and fat, and she said wished she had an abortion with me, and more. I was in tears at the words that were coming out of her mouth and the reason why it all started. She grabbed a bottle of baby lotion off my dresser and threatened to throw it at my face, so I asked her, "What are you doing? Why are you doing this?" She then had the bottle in the air to throw it, so I tried to grab it.

I should have just let her throw it at my face because she then swore that my almost 300 pound self was trying to fight her, so she ran into her room and grabbed an aluminum bat. She came back and hit me on my leg with it. It wasn't a tap; she swung and hit me. I then grabbed my phone and ran out the house with no shoes on. She grabbed my hair and told me to give her her phone. I was still trying to get away with the phone because I needed to call my dad to come get me. I had no choice but to give her the phone because my head was starting to hurt.

Once she let go, I turned around and told her I hated her. Of course, I did not mean it, but at the time I wanted her to feel the same pain that I felt. I went to a neighbor's house that's like an aunt to me and took my ponytail down. All of the braids on my left side fell to the floor. To this day, the hair doesn't grow right there.

That was it. If it had not been my senior year, I would have transferred schools and left then and there. Was this really how my winter break was starting? She called the neighbor's house the next day wanting to talk to me, but I had already gone to my grandmother's house to get my dad's number, and he was coming that night. I went to pack my clothes, and she was saying how sorry she was. Of course, I forgave her. She gave me my phone, I got my things, and I left.

February rolled around, and it was time to take my senior pictures. At the last minute, she told me she didn't want to take me because I had started getting my dress made without her the weekend before. But, she had not wanted to take me, so a friend ended up taking me. So the day of my pictures, I was dressed and ready to go. I was in tears because I had an appointment at the place. I didn't need her money. I just needed her to take me, but she wasn't budging. I walked over to another neighbor's house, who is also considered like an aunt to me, and she wiped my tears, fixed my hair because I had been sweating, and took me.

On the Thursday night before my prom, I do not remember what the disagreement was over, but again I was out of the house and at the same aunt's house who took me to take my pictures. This time I managed to take my phone. She was telling my aunt she wasn't giving me my prom dress or clothes for school the following morning. I cried myself to sleep. The next day at school, I got a call to go to the office, and I saw my cousin walking to the office as well. I went in and my mom was standing in the front to pick us up. I was so scared because I thought she was going to kidnap us or something. I got a text from my aunt saying she had to pick things up for my champagne party, and my mom was picking us up, and she was meeting us at the nail shop. We left, and my mother never mentioned anything from the previous night.

The day before I graduated, it was bad. I had all my things packed and was ready to go. My sister and I had agreed that we would both be leaving this time, but she was leaving after summer, and I was leaving after I walked the stage. I moved the morning after grad night.

So 2008 was when I moved with my dad. I went to visit frequently, and we talked all the time. We came to the realization that our relationship works better when we are not living under the same roof. There were times I visited and said I would never go back, but I couldn't stay away too long. She was always apologizing for what we had been through. I was still hurting from that because I wondered how could this person whom I love more than anyone else in this world do these things and say these things to me.

In 2010, I had to move back. I thought my life was over. I had to apply for the county and was getting $200 dollars a month and food stamps. I never in my life wanted to do that. But like people told me, it's okay if you use it as the assistance that it is. I moved back in March and started working for the post office in October and got myself off the county assistance. Things were good until she wanted me to pay so much money for things that I was always broke, even with a job.

Then the arguing started again, and I couldn't take it, so a year after I moved back, my boyfriend and I got an apartment. She was angry at first, but she got over it, and our relationship was the relationship I had always wanted from her. 2011 was the start of great things with me and her. We hung out. She would come over my house, and I would go over hers. We talked on the phone every single day. I just loved her so much, and I was finally starting to feel the love I always longed for. We still argued, but we were so much alike that it had to happen. We never fought like we did before though. We were both stubborn with bad attitudes.

We brought in the 2012 New Year together, and a few days later, I was taking her to the hospital. The lining of her stomach was gone, and the doctors blamed it on the drinking. She had stopped drinking hard liquor and was only drinking wine.

When this happened, she stopped completely because she needed to be here for her girls.

In April, she was back at the hospital, and this time they say it was a mass that didn't need to be removed because it had shrunk in the time she was there. I was enjoying my mother. There was not a day I went without talking to her. I invited her to my coworker's church for Mother's Day, and we joined the Sunday after.

My mother hadn't been to church in over five years. But then, every Sunday, my mom, my sister, and I would be at church. She wouldn't always feel good before services, but she didn't miss.

On September 10, 2012, I got the call that would change my life forever. My mom had been in the hospital over the weekend, and they were running tests. She called to tell me she had stomach cancer. I was at a loss for words. I went to my job and told them I would need the week off. I was at that hospital with her every day. The following week, they transferred her to a different hospital, and when she arrived, she told me her cancer was at Stage 4. That was the first and last time my mom saw me cry over her illness.

Though I knew how serious it was, I didn't imagine her drying. I knew we would fight this, and everything would be okay. She was at my birthday celebration October 9th. She got married October 20th. Everything was perfect. I was taking her to her chemo every other Tuesday. I didn't mind doing anything for her. One time though, we had an argument, so I missed a week of seeing her. I told her, "I think I'm crowding you, and I need to give you space because I am coming over every chance I get and calling so much."

When I went and I saw her for the first time in over a week, I couldn't believe my eyes. I stood at the door with tears in my eyes. Her face was so sunken in, and she was so small. She had been losing so much weight, and I had been seeing her so much that I was the only person who didn't notice. Then her husband was getting her dressed and bathing her, and my sister was putting her legs on and off the couch for her. It was crazy to me. This independent woman had to depend so much on people. I hated it for her.

On November 18, 2012, she asked me to take her to emergency to get a breathing treatment. I had no clue it would be the last time she rode in my car or asked me to take her somewhere. My mother Cressie Latrice Daniels-Marshall died November 20, 2012. She was still apologizing to me about our relationship until her last breath. I had forgiven her, and I didn't care about that anymore. I just didn't want her to leave me.

She was that one person that no matter what I could call and depend on for anything. She was that one person who was going to always be there. She was that one person who made sure I was always okay. But now that one person is gone. And she left me with a huge responsibility: looking after not only myself but my fifteen-year-old sister. My sister and I have gotten closer; we now have a bond that is unbreakable.

It is hard not having my mother, and this heartache can be unbearable, but I rather her be in heaven pain free than on this earth living in the pain she was in that no one knows about but her. All that we went through only made us stronger and made me the woman that I am. I wouldn't take anything back because the relationship we had in the end was perfect!!

My Mother, God's Friend

The Ormie B. Martin Story
by
Jerry G. Martin

Ormie and Her Children

A Mother's Heart

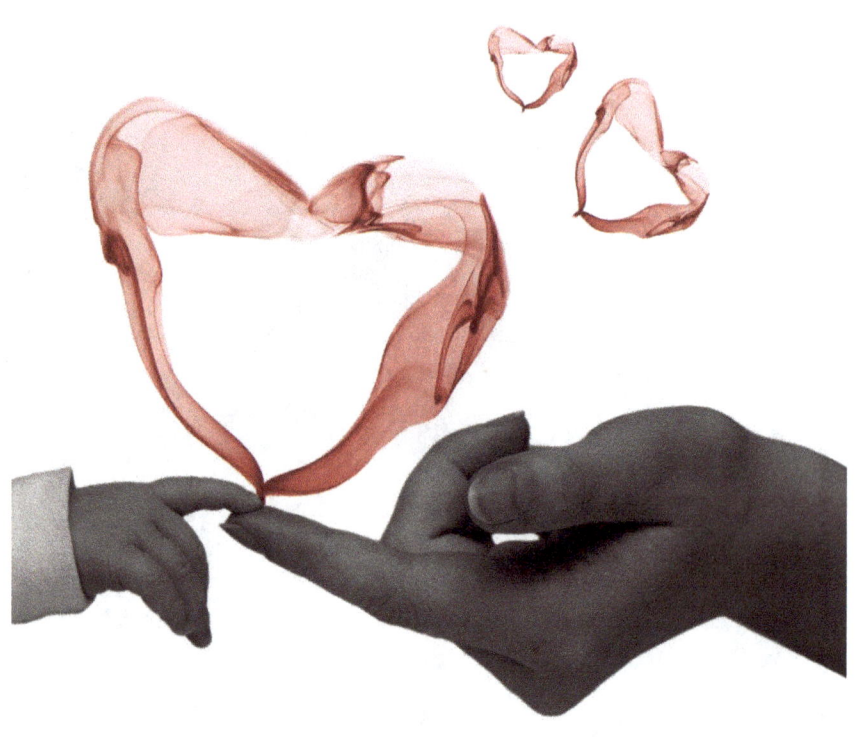

Several years ago, I was blessed to interview my grandmother Mamie Bryant. I was interested in learning some family history and insight into her life in the early 1900's. I was more interested, however, in learning about my mother, her oldest child. My mother was born in the 1920's. She is the oldest of sixteen children born to Mamie and Bishop Bryant. Her father was a hard-working dirt farmer who lived in the red dirt of East Texas. Her mother worked and did what most of the women of that day did. They worked in the fields, made quilts, canned food for the winter, washed clothes with lye soap and had a bunch of children.

They called my mother "B." I'm not sure anyone knows where that name originated. She is still called "B" by her sisters and brothers. She is called "Aunt B" by her hoard of nieces and nephews. We, my siblings and I, simply call her Momma.

Grandmother's first words to me about my mother were, "She was a nice girl, and I really mean that." She went on to say, "She got saved when she was six years old. People thought she was playing, but she really got saved." Then she said, "She really loved her daddy, and she was a big help with her sisters and brothers."

Mother was blessed to complete high school at the small segregated country school. As Mother tells it, it was her heart's desire to be a nurse. After high school, she found herself living in Oklahoma City during World War II and working at a military installation. It was in Oklahoma during the war that she met a young soldier. They met, and they married.

The first of their eight children was born in August of 1945. I came along five years later. I am the fifth child. I guess you could say things were getting crowded when I came along. From my earliest recollection, I have always felt special. I thought that special feeling was unique to me. I later discovered that Mom has an uncanny ability to make several

53

people feel special at the same time. Perhaps it was in the way that she would pull us to the side and whisper in our ear that we had a special ability or gift.

As I look back, I can see that she was bending us in the direction that she thought best utilized our personality and our abilities. Mother had a very unique perspective of her children. She saw us as a gift from God. She dedicated each of us back to God for His use and service. With that understanding, our lives revolved around church, Christian living and work. It did not take me long to realize that Mother, and Father for that matter, was totally committed to serving God. They were not committed out of a sense of duty to God, but out of their love for God.

One of the dynamic attributes of Mother is that she is a teacher. She took every opportunity to teach us lessons on life and living. She wanted us to excel at everything we undertook. When we were involved in programs at church for Christmas or Easter, she wanted us to be the best presenter. She taught us how to stand, hold our hands together, look at the audience, and speak loudly and clearly. She made us learn those speeches, even if she had to use a switch. We sang with the children's choir and were in the plays. Vacation Bible School was a must. It goes without saying that we were in Sunday School every Sunday morning and in church every time the church doors were opened.

It was important to Mother that we all had a firm foundation of Christian instruction. Her instructions and training, however, went far beyond the church. Mother had six boys before a girl was born into the family. Mother decided that she would teach us boys all the things that one would normally think would be tasks for girls. Consequently, we all had to wash clothes, clean house, and cook. Mother's idea was to teach us to be self-sufficient. I remember taking loads of clothes to the washateria. We were taught to make cornbread from scratch, cut up a chicken, fry it and make the gravy as well. By the time each of us left home, we knew how to cook for real.

Mother also had the idea that each of us would learn how to play the piano. So, off to piano lessons we went. She went all out with a real piano teacher who made us read music and perform at recitals. Mother was determined that we would be special. She received some criticism for being too strict on her boys. That did not deter her from her conviction that she had to mold us into productive citizens. While instructing us was something that she did almost daily, Mother also excelled at encouraging and assisting. She had the ability to discern the differences in our personalities. She seemed to know exactly what to say to each of us to encourage us to believe in God and to believe that we could make a difference. I was quite young when she would say, "You have wisdom, and you will be my counselor."

Even to this day, she will call me and ask my opinion on matters as her advisor. She has done so for many years. I know that she has spoken into the lives of all her children with words of encouragement. All of us have heard her voice when things were difficult. Mother has gone much further than encouraging us with her words. She is always ready to assist whenever there are times of sickness or challenges of any kind.

I believe God has honored her desire to be a nurse. She has labored tirelessly to assist ill family members and non-family members alike. If you are sick, just call her. She has a remedy in store for you. In fact, it is likely that she has some medicines, herbs, or supplements in that special closet that everyone knows where it is but will not enter. We tell her that we are going to report her to the authorities for practicing medicine without a license.

If I were asked what was most impressive about Mother, I would say it is her love and care for her family. Her husband was definitely the number one priority. Close behind is her children. Mother was always working and engaged in helping others. She was quite involved in church activities, but we were never far out of her sight. Mother got licensed as a beautician. She had my dad build a beauty shop behind our house, so she could work and watch us. She would be in the shop frying hair and at the same time would observe us trying to sneak off to play down the street. She would walk out of the shop while hair was drying to check to see if we were working on our assignments.

When everything is said about my mother Ormie B. Martin, we cannot overlook the one thing that everyone agrees on about her. She is a woman of prayer and a friend of God. My earliest memories are of Mother telling us about Jesus. She emphasized the importance of giving our lives to Him, so we could go to heaven and miss hell. She told us of the goodness of Jesus and the power of prayer. We observed how she lived her life as a model of Christian living and faith in God. When we were sick and had no health insurance, she would doctor on us and pray the prayer of faith. We saw the power of God demonstrated through her prayer and obedience. If there was one thing we knew for sure that was that God is real and He saves, heals and works on behalf of those who love Him.

During the Vietnam War, she had five sons who were eligible to be drafted and sent to the war zone. There were so many young men who were killed, maimed and psychologically damaged by that war. Mother declared, "I did not raise my sons for Uncle Sam's army to get killed, wounded and damaged. I raised them to serve in God's army." Although some of us received notices from the government to serve, none of us ever did. Mother would take those notices to God and plead her case before Him, and He heard her cry. If you would talk to her, she could tell you of miracle after miracle that God did for our family.

Mother's modeling of Christian living showed us how a wife functions under the authority of her husband with love and respect. She showed us what the God kind of love is that exemplified itself fully as she gave herself to dad's care in the latter years of his life. She showed us how to serve in the church and to follow the leadership that God placed over her. She showed us what a woman of discretion is.

There is no other mother in the world like Ormie B. Martin. All of her children have risen, and we all call her blessed. She has blessed us.

A Mother's Heart

Dr. Cassundra White-Elliott

Unconditional Love

The Franzette Kyles Story
by
Jourdan Jovel

Franzette and Jourdan

A Mother's Heart

My relationship with my mom has always been open and honest; for instance, if something was going to hurt like taking a shot, my mom would tell me about it beforehand.

My mom does not punish me because she is angry. If she is angry, she tells me to go to another room. While I am in the other room, she calms down and thinks of the right punishment. After she punishes me, she asks me if I think the punishment was fair. If my mom thinks that the punishment was wrong, she will ask for forgiveness, even if I didn't think it was wrong.

Whenever I am having a problem, I talk to my mom about it. She always seems to know what I am going through and gives great advice. She helps when it comes to school, friends, or anything really.

I know that she loves me, and she knows that I love her. Almost every day of my life, she tells me that she loves me and that she thanks God that I was born. She says that I am a gift to her.

My mom also stops whatever she is doing to spend time with me unless she is witnessing to other people because I am more important than anything else that she is doing.

When I was younger, every Friday, my mom and I always had mother-daughter days. We would go to the park, the museum, or out to fancy restaurants; it was fun every time. One time, when I was a toddler, my mom and I were at a restaurant where music was playing, and I asked my mom to dance. We danced around all of the waiters and waitresses even though there wasn't a dance floor and we weren't supposed to dance, but she loved me enough.

My mom also taught me how to skate. It has been a while since I last skated, so I am not as good. She was also teaching me how to skateboard.

She taught how to read when I was two, how to do multiplication when I was four, and how to do division when I was five. One time, I was in a school where I wasn't getting a good education, and they wouldn't let me transfer to another school district. My mom contacted every school board member, the mayor, each city council member, and those who were running for those positions. When they still wouldn't let me get transferred, she threatened to bring in the media and the president too. That was when they let me transfer. She has always been this serious about my education.

My mom also tells me her mistakes because she doesn't want to make me think that she is perfect, and she does not want me to make the same mistakes.

For almost my whole life, it has just been me and my mom. As a single mother, I think that she has done a great job raising me. My mom has also taught me to embrace and appreciate both of my heritages, as my dad is Hispanic and my mother is African American.

My mom has also brought me up in church since I was three weeks old because she wanted me to have the same spiritual foundation that she was given when she was little.

I think that my mom is smart, wise, and just amazing. She is a wonderful woman. And I want to be like her when I grow up. Sure she is not perfect, but I don't care. She is still amazing in my eyes, and I love her.

Dr. Cassundra White-Elliott

An Irreplaceable Bond

The Eyana A. (Williams) Flemister Story
by
Khalil Malik Flemister

Eyana and Khalil

A Mother's Heart

A mother's love is unlike anything on this world. The bond between a mother and her child is stronger than any metal, more complex than any puzzle, and more beautiful than any piece of art.

When you look up the definition of mother, it is simply defined as a female parent. But to me, there is much more than that to my mom. She deserves much more credit. She is a strong, caring, and independent woman, who with the help of my father, has devoted eighteen years plus to raising me. The amazing thing about Eyana Flemister is that not only is she my mother, but she is also my motivator and my teacher. Making her proud is my ultimate goal, and I won't stop until I succeed.

My dad did a great job of teaching me how to carry myself with respect and integrity as a young man, but my mom consistently reminded me that it was only the half of it, and that I also had to be a gentleman and treat women with respect and compassion. From a young age, I was taught that I was never to disrespect, hit, or call a woman out of her name.

Even though my mom is big on being a gentleman, she also stressed the importance of being independent and being able to cook, clean, and wash without having to rely on a woman, just the basics that I would need to take care of myself.

One thing my mom has a habit of doing is asking me a series of repetitive questions on a daily basis. One of them that sticks out is, "How are your grades?" Even though my grades are good, that question always gets me nervous. The fact that my mom does care about my grades and how I'm doing shows me that she wants me to succeed and get a good education. She always rumbles off, "You're going to college" and "You're going to do better than what I did." My mom is an intelligent woman. She proved to me that even with a family, work, and responsibilities she could go back to school and continue her education.

When it comes to responsibilities, my mother is on my back constantly. She tells me that I have to be on top of things because as an adult the real world won't wait for me. She tells me that she wants me to be responsible and be able to take care of myself when she's not around. We'll joke around a lot, but she'll tell me when I need to be serious and make sure my maturity is there when needed for serious situations.

When I hear my mom talk about her childhood with my grandma, I learn about all the picnics, talks, walks, and time spent and shared between them. You can hear the love and respect she has for her mother. And in my head, I have these crazy thoughts because my mother and I had all the same picnics, talks, walks, and time spent and shared between us. And I wonder if she knows that I feel the same exact way she is describing her love for her mom.

Even though I've gotten older and don't need as much in-face attention as I did when I was younger, it's still good to know my mom is still keeping an eye on me. I understand that she can't always be there like she was when I was a kid, but without that same affection here and there, even at 17 years old, I wouldn't feel the same. And I admit even though my mom doesn't feel this way, I'm truly a mama's boy!

Don't get me wrong. My mom and I have a great relationship, but everything wasn't always good. We do argue and disagree on many things, but that's just two hard-headed people who are just trying to get their point across. There have been heated arguments where foul words have been used and tears have been shed. But at the end, it has brought us closer, and we talked and expressed how we truly feel and try to get everything off our chests.

I've been playing sports all my life and usually I'm used to my having random strangers and people looking at me and spectating at my games and meets. But when I spot my mom in the stands, it's a different story. I get this sense of nervousness and panic because I don't want to disappoint her and perform badly. When she is there, I have a little more motivation to warm up a little harder, run a little faster and take the meet or game even more seriously, just because I want to make her proud. Her support and approval mean a lot to me.

Everyone knows that my mom is very protective, sometimes too protective to the point that sometimes it's nerve wrecking. I try to explain to her that she has to eventually let go and let me be, but she gives me the excuse that "I'm her baby, her only child." Even though I understand where she is coming from, I try to explain to her that I'm getting older and have to learn and experience things for myself. After telling her, still I never fail to hear a response like, "You'll understand when you have children of your own" or simply a sharp stare.

Even though she is a nice and laid-back woman, don't let that fool you. My mom always talks about how the only person you should fear is the Lord above and how she is pretty tough. At first, you think she's just talking but after hearing a few stories from her childhood, I learned that she was a tom boy and was indeed pretty tough. Take it from me, I've felt a couple of her punches, and there was some force behind them. I guess that's a good thing in helping me stay focused and disciplined. But I can say that my mom has both mental and physical toughness.

My mother always asks me if I felt that she did a good job as a mother. I can honestly say she did a great job. I mean no one is perfect, and people make mistakes, but she did everything in her will to make sure I lived a good life. With both my mom and dad in my life, it was great, and I'm grateful for that because I know a lot of kids who don't have that. I never had to live a tough life and struggle. I got things that I needed and wanted.

Yes, I got exposed to things that I would have chosen not to see, but I'm thankful that my mom and dad put in work and time for better opportunities.

Out of all my fears in life, losing my mother is the biggest. Just thinking about it scares me. It is a concept I can't grasp yet. You have the saying, "You don't know what you have until it's gone" and it's true. I know I have taken her for granted so many times, and I realized how much I need and depend on her being here. My dad may be the back bone of my family, but my mother is our rock and the glue that holds us together. I've learned to enjoy the little things that come with my mother and try to make the best memories possible.

I'm surprised that I had the guts to actually talk about our relationship. I'm to say that Eyana Alicia Flemister is my mother. I know it may sound cliché, but I feel that I have the best mom in the world. I'm glad that I was blessed with someone who truly loves and cares for me. And I know I can talk and confide with her and no judgment will be passed. I can count on her to be there and have my back no matter how bad the situation is. Hopefully, when she reads this, she'll recognize how much I love, care, and need her in my life.

Dedication to My Mother

Dear mother of mine, this is an ode to you.
Seventeen years and I still can't understand how a mother can care for her child like you do.
To be there, to care, like you do.
To guide and love like you do.
That warm embrace can force any storm away.
And things return to normal like they are supposed to.
I'm not just trying to rhyme or waste time.

Because each word was chosen because they perfectly describe you.
The jokes, your laugh, and that motherly affection that brightens up my day as they're supposed to
One day, I hope you open your eyes and realize that I wear my heart on my sleeve for you
I took my emotions and feeling and mixed in admiration and came up with this ode to you.

A Mother's Heart

Forgiveness

The Francine Duff Story
by
Audrey Albrecht

A Mother's Heart

I woke up to a cloudy morning, a Saturday lost as the storm came in. Outside, I could feel the stillness. Opaque clouds hung closely to the horizon. This was not a day for unpacking as I had hoped for.

How could this be? I am now fifty-something. Yet, I still avoid a truth which lives quietly around my perceived reality.

My Francine, I am ashamed to admit that this is one of the few times I have written your name since I cannot remember when. After shuffling two small boxes from storage to garage for over the past eight years, I now am a captive of the weather and forced to look inside. No more moving it along. My husband and I have moved into our dream house. I intend to deal with you there, to finally love you.

My dad Leslie was the Mother Teresa of men. But his flaw was that he loved without any rules when it came to "her." Both my parents were of strict Latin Catholic backgrounds. They found common ground in their faith when they married. Dad was shy and once told my uncle that he decided to marry her because no one else would. How silly, Dad.

It was the 1950's; the plan for women was to marry, have a baby, and be happy. Define happy when you are unsure of who you are. She was so beautiful. He was defenseless.

At seven or eight years old, I began to understand that some things just would never change. My sister, two years old than I, catered to my mom more than I did out of self-preservation. My feisty nature was not good. I am the child of a chemically dependent person. I am the grandchild of co-dependent grandparents. My mom's parents looked away from her behavior. In doing so, they ruined her and all of us too. It was out of love as most co-dependency is.

Another portable meatloaf brought over by my grandparents and dishes done, away they went. And I was left there alone as she slept throughout my childhood. However, in her moments of being awake, she could be very difficult with which to engage. So most of the time, I spoke my mind and paid the price.

From time to time, I could hear my dad talking to his mom on the phone behind a half-closed door. He would say, "Mom, she does not want to do anything, except sleep. She throws rages if I don't do what she wants." It was as if he justified her behavior.

We rarely saw my dad's parents. I know he missed them as well as his brothers and sister. To my dad, that was the longest 50 miles away imaginable. Every family event, baseball game and holiday was a struggle. We always knew who would win.

In 1969, when man finally walked on the moon, my dad lost his parents only forty days apart. That loss changed the game again. He no longer had a tether to comfort him. It was just him and me. I begged him to leave Easter of 1970. He said that he would not. God would disapprove. That was the day I knew nothing would ever change.

Shock treatments were popular at that time. Francine had thirty of them. Whatever energy and original self may have existed in her was dumbed down. There was not much left. She was a drug seeker in failing health.

Seven years had passed without much change. By then, my dad has divorced her twice and remarried her again. Was God angry? If He wasn't, we were. I was ready to leave. I met my first husband. We married in three months' time.

The first day I went to meet my future in-laws, I must have looked like a homeless person: unmatched and poor. We drove into the driveway of their beautiful home. I did not want to go. I was too embarrassed and timid. So, I sat on the porch. From the window I say Trudy, my mother-in-law to be. She was very in charge, very organized and very German. There she was, a mom, up and running. It was a little intimidating, yet fascinating. There she was doing all the 'mom' things and so filled with love for her family. In my heart, she was my first mom.

World War II was just another war; she was good at survival. She and a group of women walked from city to city in hope of finding food and shelter for two years. She was just a teenager living from day to day.

When my husband and I returned from our honeymoon, a drunk driver hit us head on going the wrong way on the freeway. Suddenly, I saw myself looking down from above. I was not in pain. My body lay there. *I must be dead,* I thought. At that moment, I heard an unspoken voice. It said that I could let go. There was peace beyond definition. That I do remember. In that moment, I knew our Creator in a way that sitting in a pew could never accomplish. In that time of twilight, I stayed in the Lord's care. I survived the crash, but I experienced brain trauma. I could not remember my husband or my name.

In the months that followed, Trudy took care of me. My in-laws took me out of the hospital. Hospitals to Trudy were places to die. She was determined to make me whole again.

Over the course of three years, she never let me down. We started with the basics: to walk, to remember and feel independent again. To this day, I have the utmost respect for her and her enduring love and patience. It has helped me to be a better mother, friend and person.

As I open Francine's boxes, I found the remnants of a scared and confused person. I looked through the Prayer books, loose ends and emptiness. I always felt guilty for loving Trudy more. I now can say it is not more love but more respect. In my life, I parented a parent and buried the emotional child that she was. But I am strong because of Trudy.

If you can love the things that are not perfect in life, you will find forgiveness. All moms aren't perfect. Love is a peace grantor, the way time is a healer.

Dr. Cassundra White-Elliott

The Strength of One Woman

The Mary Ann Vines Story
by
Cathy Vines-Nichols

Mary and Her Children

A Mother's Heart

Mary (a.k.a. May) is the oldest of eight children. Her mother's name was Rosie Gullett. Her father's name was Seaborn Henderson, Jr. They met and married, and that union produced a baby girl they named Mary Ann Vines. She grew up in Texarkana, Texas and attended school there. Mary had two children: a daughter Joyce Anderson and a son Wayne Pittman.

Later in life, she met Roger Vines, Sr. They married and eleven children were added to their family. I bless God for a mother that has endured hardship going through life's journey. 'Going through' is what made her the tree that stands by the river of living water. Her roots go deep into the soil; her soil is her children and family. It is in her strength that we have been able to stand because of the prayers she and our father prayed. I remember the prayer was, "God, save all my children. Don't let one be lost. Keep them covered with your Holy Ghost in Jesus' name, Amen."

Mary is a prayer warrior, one that fights the good fight of faith. She has never given up on her family. She is all about family. She is that strong tower in her family, the oldest of eight. The number eight represents "one who abounds in strength' is "superabundant and fertile"; she is "oil." Eight as the day was over and above this perfect completion. Mary is a blessing to her thirteen children: (in order) Joyce Montgomery, Pastor Wayne Pittman, Rosie Marie Harvey, Roger Vines, Jr., Ronald Vines, Evang. Cathy Vines-Nichols, Renee Vines, Tonie L. Vines, Melenia J. Vines, Kenneth D. Vines, Angela Vines (a.k.a. Love-Love), Kevin Vines, and the baby Ruthie Vines-Ruffin.

Mary is loyal to her family. Her trust is in the Lord. She is giving and will give you her last. She wants nothing but the best for her family. When there is a change in the atmosphere of her family, she is on it. She mixes no words in setting order (she speak what is on her mind, right or wrong). She will be heard.

Mary has the love and respect of her siblings: (in order) Albert Henderson, Justine Smith (a.k.a. Tina), Helen Williams (a.k.a. Aunt Boo), Dr. Francis Henderson-Solomon, James Henderson, Larry Henderson, and Willie Henderson. Mary, her sister Justine, and her brother Albert were very close. When Mary was moving to another part of town, it wasn't long before Tina and Albert would follow. They lived at least no more than five to ten minutes away from each other.

They did everything together. Mary and Tina were best friends. A day never went by without them calling each other on the phone. They would talk about three times a day just to hear each other's voice. They partied together. They could party, and Mary was a dancer. Oh!! this sister could hold her own. They shopped together. If the store had layaway, it was on. Back then, there was Swans in Oakland and Capwell's Department Store. Back then, layaway was a good thing. Remember, she had thirteen children. Mary and her sister even dressed alike from the top to the tip of the shoes. They could not have been any closer. That is the love of one another in the family. They were two peas-in-a pod; they laughed and cried together.

And then a shift happened. Tina started going to Ephesians Church of God in Christ on 132nd St. in Los Angeles, CA where the pastor was Bishop E. E. Cleveland. A lady by the name of Mother Ellis was the cause of Tina changing her life. Tina became a prayer warrior and that pulled Mary in. Just like they partied together, they never lost a beat. They took their love for each other to the House of Worship. They dressed, danced (shouted), praised the Lord, and lifted up hands together in worship; they sang in the choir together, and I tell you Mary can sing. They shared so much love between the two of them until God had need of Tina to come home. And the way Mary handled it was as if she was walking and holding the hand of

Jesus Himself. Yes, she cried; the tears flowed, each day for years, but Mary had thoughts of her sister; best friend was gone.

I saw in her a strength that just illuminated when she entered my presence. I now see what took her through- knowing the Christ. I watched her brother Albert and the relationship they have to this day. It is still the same each day- a phone call or a visit to one's home for dinner or driving to the mall just to sit or walk around with each other. Uncle Albert used to come over to our house every day after work just to see May (Mary). He would stay for hours. They would embrace each other, laugh and talk. Then, Albert would walk to the driveway, lift the car's trunk open and play his music, etc. Then, he would go home. This was an everyday thing. That is love in action to this day.

Mary has a love that goes beyond mother, wife, friend, daughter, aunt, and cousin. What respect her sisters and brothers have for her. Mary is still that way toward her family, even when her brother James was called home. She displayed the strength of God when she once again was going through life without another sibling. But God showed Himself strong in her.

She had her own battle with breast cancer in 1999; she is a walking testimony. I get great joy when I see my mother go forth in praise. I remember her sitting on the side of her bed with a Bible in hand reading. Mary is a strong woman of faith, integrity, and strength. Our mother is the strength of the family. Yes, she can be strong willed at times, but you have to love her! LOL! I remember the love that she shared with her oldest grandson (my son) Edgar. Their relationship was a good one. He would call her and visit. They even went to church together. They would go out to dinner and do things together. When she heard that Edgar was in the hospital, she made the journey to Las Vegas, NV to be with him.

When she entered his room, I could see the love she had for him and the compassion of her grandson for her. At her seventy-fifth birthday party, he did a tribute in dance to her. It was awesome. In the hospital, the tears flowed and the hugs came. They talked and laughed for a while just because she has such love for her family. She had made it a point to be there for him. I bless God because she made the difference that day; the love gleamed from her eyes as she looked at him, and he was smiling back at her because Granny was there. Oh the joy she brought to him.

Two days later, he died. Yet again, the strength she has never failed her. What a woman! Oh just to be a woman like her! God will give you what you need when you need it. The joy she shared with him can't be replaced. Our mother is a woman of wisdom, integrity, strength. I see this the more I put pin to paper. There are fine qualities God has placed in her to give to her family. She really is all about family. She is the rock of this family.

For her sister Francis, Mary was sister and mother. When Francis was about 17 years of age, she lived with May. She treated me with love and like her own child, and whatever she said she meant and meant what she said. I remember her cooking, washing, cleaning, and praying for her family every day. She loves her family. All I can say is that she is the greatest sister/mother that anyone could ever have. I can see the great qualities she possesses that came down from our mother; our mother was a great woman of strength. My mother also had a strong mother, who lived to 94 years of age. She never turned anyone away who was in need. Rosie, my grandmother, was a woman of wisdom and integrity. She as the rock of stability kept us coming back to the center, which is family. Because of my grandmother, my mother is who she is, and I love my mother dearly.

Dr. Cassundra White-Elliott

Mommy and Me

The Wanda Clayton Story
by
Akayla Clayton

Wanda and Akayla

A Mother's Heart

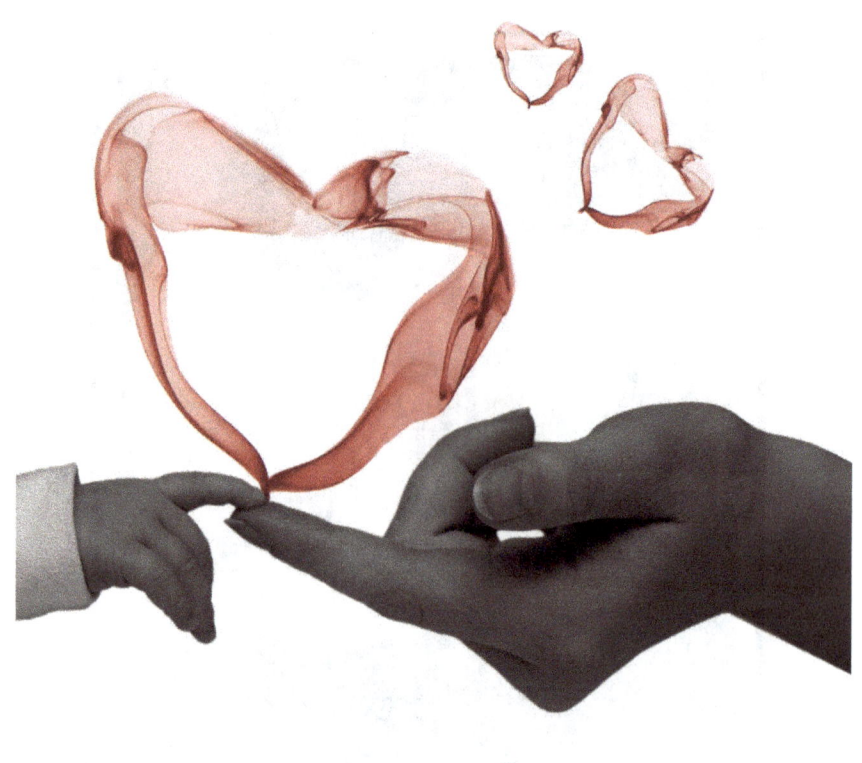

My mother and I have the best relationship ever. Don't get me wrong. It wasn't always as good as it is now, but it was never bad.

I was the second child born to my parents, four years after my brother. From the beginning, when my parents asked my brother if he liked me, he answered, "Yes." Then, he was asked what he wanted to do with me. His reply was, "Throw her in the trash." He eventually changed his mind and became my big brother!

While growing up, I was always a 'daddy's girl' and my brother was a 'mommy's boy.' My mom and my brother would do things together, and my dad and I would do things together. I always knew she loved me, but I didn't think I was her favorite.

When we were growing up, my mom was the most youthful, laid back, smartest, prettiest thing I had ever encountered. She never looked or acted like the other mothers in the neighborhood. While those moms were getting old, mommy was staying young by skating in the street with us, riding bikes with us, even posing as a teenager attending summer day camp with us!! Mommy didn't work full time until I was in fourth grade, so she spent a lot of time volunteering at my school. The teachers treated me differently/better I feel because my mom was so involved.

My mom was an LVN and worked through a registry per diem. She didn't get benefits, vacation or 401k, but she made good money. One day, my parents were having a discussion about that, and my dad bet her that she couldn't get a full-time job and earn a vacation. Of course, she responded that she could. She went out the next day and got one. She became employed at the phone company. Boy ole boy did she prove him wrong!! Mommy has remained employed for twenty-nine years and counting. Her work ethic is impeccable. She is the perfect example of hard work and dedication. She worked split shifts in the beginning. She would drop me off at school, go to work, pick me up, feed me and drop me off at home, and then head back to work.

Mommy taught me so much about life, instilling certain values and morals in me at an early age. She is always the "cup half full person," never negative and always willing to help. She also started working on building my self-esteem early on. By me being a plus size girl, Mommy always made sure I was dressed appropriately and was comfortable with my height, weight and over-all look. She never let me walk around with my shoulders hunched and my head down. I was the best thing since sliced bread in my household, so when I was in the world nothing anyone said to me or about me even mattered because I was a SUPER STAR to my mother.

My mom told me everything that she knows about life, including finances, the importance of good credit, relationships, sex, employment, etc. If she knew it, she taught it. She was the best teacher not only to me and my brother, but to our friends as well. She would have reading sessions with us and the neighborhood kids sitting on the porch. We lived in Compton, so sometimes she would have the most treacherous gang bangers in "the hood" reading a book, asking how to pronounce a word and feeling that they could do or be something other than what they were at that time just because of the attention and concern for them that Mommy showed.

With all the things that Mommy taught and showed me, I still chose to grow up and do things my way. My mother never made me feel bad about the things that I did or the paths that I was choosing. She would always help me through it and re-educate me on her previous lessons. I never remember her telling me "I told you so" or throwing my mistakes in my face. She would never chastise me in front of others. Even if I was wrong, we maintained a united front when others were around. Behind closed doors she would tell me I was wrong and discipline me accordingly. Even when I was married, my husband would 'tell on me.' He used to say the reason I acted like that is because she thought everything I did or said was cute. It wasn't that at all, but she would never express her dislike for those things in front of him, but she would definitely let me know about myself when it was just her and me.

Mommy made everything an adventure growing up. We never had to be concerned about finances, living arrangements or any adult issues. We never knew that money was tight at times until we were young adults. We thought that spending a day at the beach or park with a picnic lunch was a treat, not knowing money was low. Getting in the car and riding down streets and learning directions and landmarks was fun, but those were probably the times when there wasn't a lot of money to do other things. We never even knew on some of our road trips that we were lost. Mommy was too cool to let that show. All we knew is we were spending quality time with Mommy.

Mommy has always been bad with paying bills on time. When I was younger, sometimes I would come home from school and the phone would be cut off. I would go to a neighbor's house and call her at work, and she would say "It's right here in my purse with a stamp on it. Let me go downstairs and pay it." When she would let our lights get cut off, she would make the best of it. We would have a candlelight dinner and a candlelight bath. It would be the best. But come on now, how many times is that going to be fun. It would have been different if we didn't have the money, but to have the money and not pay had just become to be too much for me. She showed me how to pay bills, make our doctor and dentist appointments, travel arrangements and passed the torch to me when I was about thirteen.

After a certain age, my brother and my father started doing their own thing freeing up both Mommy's and my time allowing us to spend more time together. We started being best friends. If you saw Mommy, you saw me. We did and still do everything together. We ride to work, church, the nail shop, and the grocery store and travel and live together. We are the best roommates anyone could ask for. We help each other and respect each other's privacy and feelings.

There is never a time that I can think of that I needed my mother and she was not there. Whether I was celebrating or mourning, she was there. When my daughter was born, Mommy was right there. When my daughter passed away, Mommy was right there. When my father died, Mommy was right there. When my husband died, needless to say, Mommy was right there. I recently had major surgery, and I didn't think it was possible, but the way she took care of me made me love her even more.

I tell her all the time that I wish I could share her with other people because I am so so so lucky to have her. She brightens my days in the best kind of ways just by hearing her voice or seeing her smile. It is so comforting to know that there is someone in this world that genuinely loves me, respects, supports and wants the best for me. I wish everyone was as lucky as I am, and I thank God that He chose someone so special to be my #1 fan and supporter, my teacher, my doctor, my counselor, my protector, my rainbow after the storm, my MOTHER.

Dr. Cassundra White-Elliott

Through it All, I'm Still Standing

The Diane Jackson Story
by
Dalejuan Jackson

A Mother's Heart

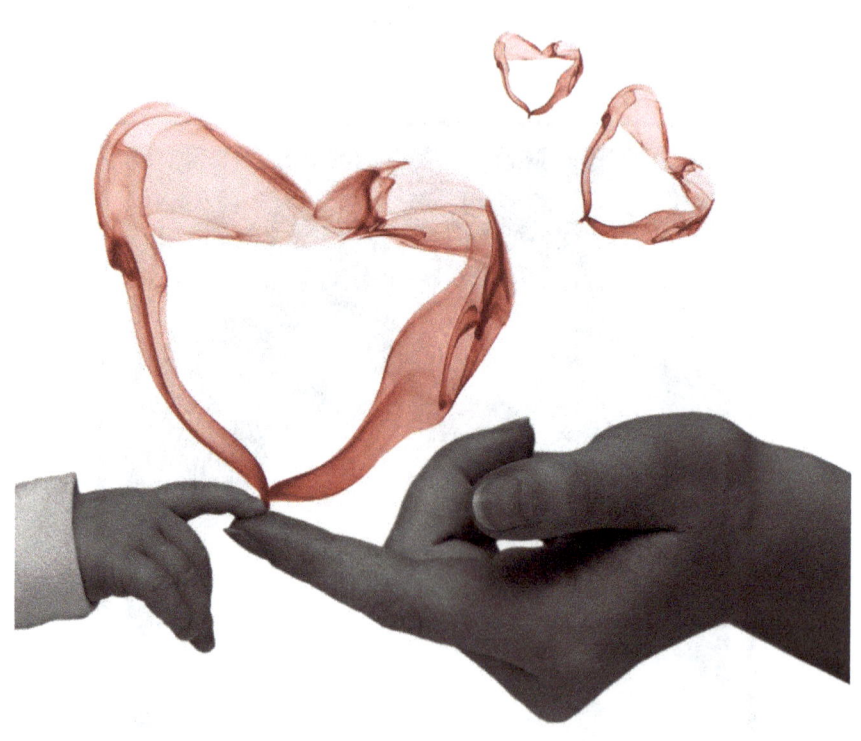

My name is Dalejuan. I am seventeen years old. And I want to tell you how my life has been with my mother Diane Jackson for seventeen years. She is the greatest mother in the world to me. My mom and I have a very outstanding relationship.

In the beginning of 2004 was the first time I had ever experienced been scared. I almost lost my mother. She is the closest person to me. All I can remember is my sisters trying to hide something from me. My sisters were talking to each other, and I had heard crying and them saying Mama had been shot two times and she might not make it. I lay on the bed and cried. I also prayed myself to sleep, asking God, "Please don't let my mother die." My mother told and promised me when she got shot that she would leave the street life alone. It took my mom about five months to walk straight again. I never felt hurt like this before in my life. I thank God for my mom because she is still here today.

I learned how to pray and believe in God and have faith because my mom has always kept me in church as long as I can remember. Even when my mom was living the street life, she always made sure that I was in church every Sunday morning. I love my mom, and I am very thankful for her. No matter what she has done before in her life, my mama loves me and wants the very best for me. She raised me to be the nice young man that I am today. My father, whom I miss a lot, was a great father up to his death. My dad took very good care on me. Also, he made sure I had everything I needed and wanted. But, my mom taught me everything that I know. She is the one that keeps me dressed very nicely. My mother has always bought me nice clothes. During my whole life, my mom has always taken very good care of me.

My mom is the greatest gift I can ever have in my life. From the day I was born to present day, she has been by my side protecting me from the dangers of the earth. My mom Diane has given me the gift of life, and I want to dedicate this story to the greatest woman in my life.

During my childhood, my mom and I had the best of times as we did everything together, such as go to the park or go to watch a movie at the theatre. My mom is the greatest person in the world because she knows what to say and when to say it. When I was going through hard times, she was there to comfort me and say it was okay to feel that way and everything would be all right. My mom has been there through everything, such as a bloody nose to having a family member pass away in my life. She takes care of me every day and cares about me like no one else in the world can. She feeds me, gives me a place to live, and will love me no matter what happens on this earth.

The day I was born, my mom held me in her arms, and she has never let go since. She protects me from going in the wrong direction in life and keeps me grounded and moving forward. She helps me decide what's wrong from right and what is good for me and how I can improve every day. Diane is the best mom a son can have. She will go great lengths to protect her baby and do anything to keep me safe. She can be loving when I need her to, as well as being protective when it's needed. My mom is my best friend because I can tell her everything without being judged. She listens to me and gives me advice better than a therapist can do. She can turn the darkest days into a bright day in just minutes. She is my all, and I will do everything for her as well. I will also protect her from danger and do anything through the end of time.

My mom, Diane is also the greatest cook I know. She cooks anything that I can think of, and it is delicious. It is better than a restaurant or any of my other family members. She can be the world's greatest chef by a long slide. Diane is the best at everything. Cooking, working, and loving, she can do it all with ease. My mom can have a bad day or two and still have powerful words to say to make anyone's day brighter. Every day, she stays strong for people who count on her to be a great example. She is my hero because she stays strong and moves on from all the hardships she has to deal with in her life. She never shows what problems she has and keeps moving forward to better her life. She will always be my hero, my mom, and the best person in the world. Diane will stay strong and be in my heart until the end of time. No matter what happens, I will always love her and be there to guard her through any dangers or adversity. She has protected me throughout my life, and I will do the same for her no matter what it takes. My mom is my whole life, and I will do anything for her.

During my whole life, my mom Diane has done more for me than I can imagine. She has cared for me even though we have some arguments once in a while. Even though sometimes we don't connect on everything, we will always be best friends and love each other. Together, we make a perfect team, and we do everything together. That's why we are best friends.

My mom is the most beautiful woman on this earth. She is a goddess in her own right. She can shine light in the midst of the darkness. Diane can walk past someone and make him or her feel like a brand new person. She can talk to people and change their lives by giving them advice to better their lives. My mom gives advice to my family, and they come out better people. She is really a life changer and a good person inside and out. Diane is an angel that is alive on earth that has been sent from the heavens to protect and guide me. She is here to give me my own wings and send me on the right path in life. Everywhere she goes, she sets fireworks off and has a great smile to make everyone happy. My mom is better and greater than any celebrity or more beautiful than a rose. She will climb any mountain to see a better destination. Even if she is not rich in money, she is always rich with love, and she will spread the wealth to anyone who wants it.

My mom has the voice of an angel when she sings in the church with the choir. She is very is close to God. She loves God, and I know God loves her even more. She prays every night for a stronger and better day tomorrow, and God grants her wish. Diane is the heart and soul in my family, and she is truly a gift from God. My mom will be in my life way after she is gone from the earth, and I will never forget about what she has done for me. I will always have the greatest memories with her, and I will create more in the future as well.

She is not the most famous, but she is a star in my eyes. She shines brightly and leads the way to heaven. My mom is the apple of my eye and is the greatest mom a child can have. She will pick me up when I fall and clean me up when I'm dirty. My mom is the one I can count on to help with my ideas or protect me from harm. Diane will love me when I start my own family and when she will have more grandchildren. And when she does, she will love them the same way she loves me.

When I was young, my mom took me places to make memories and enjoy life together. We went to the beach where my mom and I built sandcastles and swam in the ocean. We dug holes in the sand and jumped in there as if we were trying to find treasures. Pretending we were pirates, we ran with fake swords and tried to talk funny. She also took me to watch plenty of movies at the theatre like *Finding Nemo, Peter Pan*, and more. We went almost every weekend, and we still go occasionally. We also did arts and crafts, like drawings or making birdhouses while reading kids stories together. We read many books written by Dr. Seuss, but my favorite is *Sam I Am*. We also read poems that were funny and exciting also written by Dr. Seuss.

During my first year of school, my mom was the first one I would count on to help me with my homework and my projects. When a problem was too hard or a project was too messy, my mom would come and help me out with no cost. She would participate in all of my fundraisers and go to all of my school events. My mom would do all she could to help me succeed in school, and she still does today. Without my mom, I don't know where I would be and what I would be doing today. My mom wants me to succeed in life because she has seen people go the wrong way in life, and she wants me to be a better person. Diane is the love of my life, and she means the world to me. I would do anything to protect her from any danger we come across in this world.

My mom is the best woman in the world simply because she gives without expecting anything back. She gives all she can to help people in the time of need, and she does it just because she knows that it is the right thing to do and because God has sent her on this earth to help people. She helps people because she knows it's hard for people, and she wants to do as much as she can. She gives great advice and amazing speeches to change people for the better. She also will listen to your problems and say what is needed and will not hold back. My mom will change a person's life in just five minutes.

Great parents love their children unconditionally, and that's what my mom does. Even if she doesn't know you, she won't judge you, but love you. She doesn't pick on all your flaws, but gives you pointers to improve. My mom loves anyone she comes across even if you don't do the same. She is kind hearted and is a blessing sent on earth. She can relate to you in many ways, and you can talk to her for hours about anything. My mom will amaze you in a thousand ways and entrance you with her knowledge. In my opinion, her heart might be the biggest one on this earth. She expects nothing, but she will give everything to you. My mom says that it is her mission on this earth to help people better their lives. Diane has been there for all who need a shoulder to cry on or an extra hand for help. She will always be pure and heavenly even through all the sins around her.

When you need a friend, my mom will be the best one. My mom is my best friend simply because she understands me like no one else can. She knows when I'm sad and need someone to talk to or when I'm tired and I need an extra blanket. She will be there to talk about what happened in school or help me with an extremely hard math problem. She knows what to do when I'm up late thinking about a past family member or where to go to calm me down when I need a rest. She is a goddess that will spread her wings to fly you to your destination or simply protect you from evil. Diane is a great mom as well as a great friend to have in my life.

Chasing her dreams is something she does constantly. Her dream is to have her son grow into a man, and she is doing a wonderful job. Her dream is to see me succeed as well as improve the world around her. She has affected my life greatly because she has guided me in the right direction. She has set my priorities straight and has made me a better man. She has given me the gift of life, and I want to give her the gift of love. I love her because she will love me back. Diane is a seed who has blossomed into a beautiful rose. She is still growing in knowledge and will keep growing just like I am. My mom is faithful and respectful in everything she does, and that's why everyone loves her.

All in all, I have witnessed an angel on this earth, and I know it is my mom. She has been sent down to guide me to my destination as well as help people through every single thing. My mom is indescribable, but I would like to come close to saying she is amazing.

Mommy

The Esperanza Jones Green Story
by
Quantanique S. Williams

Esperanza and Her Children

A Mother's Heart

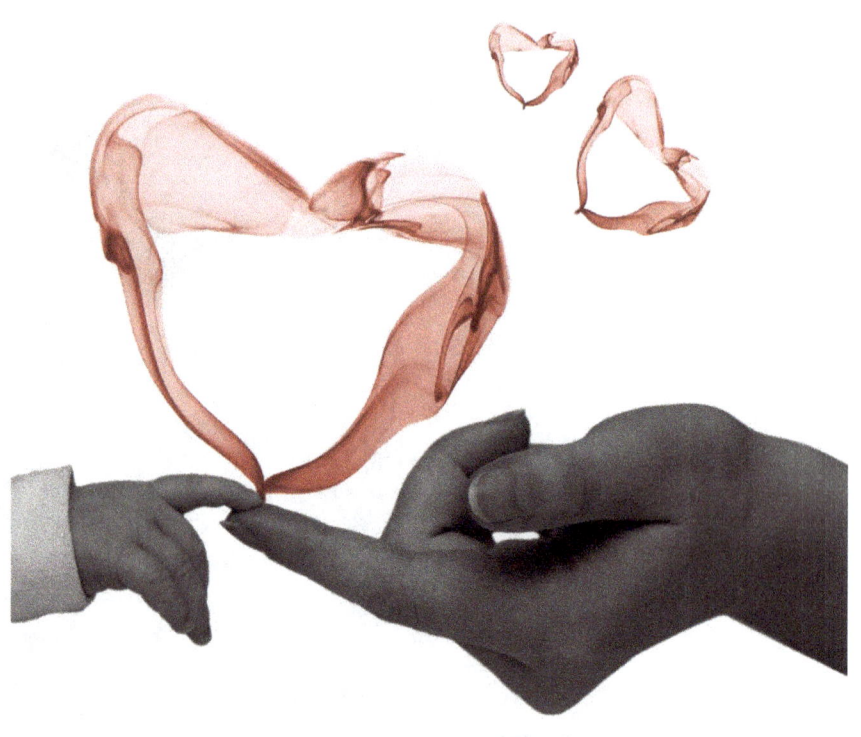

My relationship with my mother is one that has grown in recent years, and her wisdom is something I need more than ever before as I'm now walking into motherhood. Just being pregnant and thinking of having to actually birth to this little person gives me a great respect for my mother for just deciding to bring me into this world at the young age of seventeen.

My mother has always been affectionate hugging, kissing and sharing her love through not just words, but actions, by always making sure my siblings and I were fed, well-groomed and clothed.

What I admire most about my mother is her compassion for the less fortunate and the homeless. She is never ashamed to eat among them or give what she has to others. She serves in her community.

My mother taught me to never half do any task I take on whether it was a chore she told me to do, school work or a project I was working on. She taught us never to be racist and to embrace all others.

I love my mom's creativity. I remember always walking to Michael's Arts & Craft store with her when I was a young child. Now she beads and bakes all types of neat things.

Something I don't understand was why she didn't make visitation available to my father for three years when they were going through a divorce. Did she think of herself or did she have me and my sister Kierra in mind? I often wonder why she didn't have that one-on-one talk about puberty or what they call the bird-and-bees conversation with me. Did she feel uncomfortable? Did she not know how to because her mother was gone?

Something I'd like to do differently is actually have that conversation formally but casually with my child about his different stages in life, from the change of the body, to change of hormones, to the feeling of liking the opposite gender. I'd like to discuss clear expectations I have for him and instill the Lord in him at a young age. I'd like to be a woman who is content with being alone and that speaks up for herself and doesn't allow anyone male of female to talk to me any type of way. I dislike that my mother seems to do this and continues to stay, and I found myself in the same place years later.

My mother always encouraged my goals and supported my talents. I never felt ashamed of my artistic goals.

Esperanza Moreno Jones now Esperanza Moreno Green is my mother. I love her very much, and I'm thankful for her unconditional love and support.

Dr. Cassundra White-Elliott

The Love I Have for My Mother

The Vertie Mae McClinton Story
by
Millicent (McClinton) Redd

A Mother's Heart

I am thanking God right now for my mother. She is still here with us today at seventy-two years of age, coming up to seventy-three in July 2013.

Some of my sweetest memories of my mother center on fragrances. Our home was fragrant too, as she aired the house regularly, scrubbed the interior with pine cleaners throughout the rooms. A frequent memory I treasure is of my mom hanging clothes on the line to absorb the outdoor freshness. I can see her stretching to reach the clotheslines, as wooden clothespins filled her apron pockets and a few clamped between her teeth.

But I think the best smell was Mom's cooking early in the morning before we would get up. I remember one morning she decided to make something new for breakfast. She was happy about her new dish. Momma made fried potatoes with chopped green onions and scrambled eggs that had onions and another veggie. When we came into the dining room to eat, we all looked! What in the world is that Momma made? Looking at her face, with a big smile on it, we all decided to eat what Momma had prepared. She was so happy. At the end of the day, that is what mattered.

My first impression of my mom is the unconditional love that she has for all of us, just like Jesus. There are five children total in our household. Jesus has the same love for us, never wanting us to go in the wrong direction or making unwise decisions. That is how my mom was, and today, she is still the same way. That reminds me of this song, "Jesus loves me, and this I know, for my mother shows me so."

Momma never considered it a sacrifice to stay home with us while we were small. I am sure having five children at home was quite a handful; however, she never complained. I think at times it must have been difficult, but she always made sure all our needs were met.

I can remember when I was in junior high school, and it was coming to graduation time and my sister and I wanted to look different from the other girls. So our mother decided to make our graduation clothes, and we were the best-looking girls there. Everyone was saying how good we looked, not knowing that our mother made our graduation outfits. Another fun memory while we were in high school is our classmates thought my mother was our older sister. We never told them otherwise. Our weekend family outings with our mother and father, who has gone home to be the Lord, included going to Knott's Berry Farm, playing baseball in the park and sometimes in the yard, hearing Momma telling Daddy not to throw the ball so hard at us because we're girls. Momma always looked out for us.

During my father's illness, almost every evening was spent with the sound of my mother's well-modulated voice reading or singing to my father. I remember her sitting by his bed next to the lamp while Dad lay there looking so peacefully. Mom's gentle seriousness, coupled with her genuine appreciation of Dad was awesome to see. I saw it every time Mom's mouth began to work in that special way of hers that always culminates in helpless laughter.

Now, it's our turn to look out for Momma. All we have now is Momma. My momma is one of my best friends even though we don't see eye to eye. I love her with all my heart. When she is not feeling well, I am praying for her, always asking the Lord to give her long life on this earth.

My mom and dad really loved the Lord with all their hearts. I thank the Lord for them. Back in 1978, they went to a church called Love, Peace and Happiness Church. On the next night, they invited me and my sisters and brother to go. Now my mom is a little up in age, so she really doesn't drive anymore. So, every Sunday morning, we ride together to the house of the Lord. This is the best gift of all- to see my mother in the house of the Lord. Thank you, Lord.

A Mother's Heart

Dr. Cassundra White-Elliott

A Mother Like None Other

The Mercer Yvonne McClinton Story
by
Ahleeyah Nichols

Mercer and Ahleeyah

A Mother's Heart

I love my mom, but I don't even know where to start to describe the love and way I feel about my mother. My mom is Mercer Yvonne McClinton, and she is the best mother I could ever have. My mom is loving, kind, gentle, caring, and many more words I can describe her with. My mom has been through many trials and tribulations during her life, and as a result, she is a very strong and humble woman.

My mother has always taught me to keep God first in my life. While growing up, we would go to Love, Peace, and Happiness Church every Sunday. She taught me to keep God first because we need Him in our lives, and with God, anything is possible. I was taught that God would always get me through any situation even if I thought it was impossible.

No one in all my eighteen years of living has nurtured and encouraged me more than my mom. There has never been anyone there who comforted me more than my mom or has been there for me through my early adult years like my mom. The value I owe my mom is incalculable, but my love and appreciation for my mother is the best gift I can give her each day. My mom is not perfect. I know her faults and weaknesses, but they seem so small to me because of her great and positive influence in my life. My mom has taught me well and pointed me in the right path for life, and that overshadows any of her imperfections.

My mom has had a direct influence on my life, and I always took what she said into consideration, even if I didn't agree. My mom has had an influence in my life, and because of her influences, she is the only person I go to when I have questions or just want to talk. Because I have lived with my mom, we have always had a close bond. Each day when I got in from school, we would just sit and talk and have many heart-to-heart conversations. My mom knows I love her with all my heart; I would do anything for my mother.

A Mother's Heart

My mom and I have been through so much throughout my life. She has taught me to be a strong young lady. When my father passed away, my mom was there to comfort me each and every day. My mom would let me know each day would get easier. Sometimes, we would just sit and reminisce about all the wonderful times we had together as a family. After my dad passed away, my mom bought me a jewelry box that said "Love" on it and Bible scriptures that went along with love. I loved the fact that she gave me that gift because the scriptures helped me to cope with my loss. Inside the gift box, I put the flowers from my dad's casket as a keepsake.

I think since I'm genetically part of my mom, I automatically have some qualities just like her. Growing up watching my mom do things could have also had a powerful impression on me too. My mom likes many things, like reading, music and movies; I have those same likes, and I know they were passed on in my genes. My mom loves good music like Jazz, and she love Robin Thick and Eric Benet. In my family, she is known for bumping Jazz music super loudly.

As her daughter, I have some type of musical talent; I have an ear for music, and I like everything loud no matter what I am listening to. My mom passed down a gift of writing to me, and both my mom and I are very good at it. She reads everything, like magazines, books, and newspapers, etc., and she writes plays.

Her life is like someone who found avenues for personal growth. My mom always thought and taught me there is room for improvement. She taught me how to take corrective criticism and told me it is good to be quiet. I appreciate everything my mom has done for our family. Raising two kids, washing, ironing, cleaning, and cooking isn't always an easy job when you're a single parent; it takes a lot of time and energy, but through it all, she still found time to read, which gave her peace and helped her to relax.

The thing that amazes me is through her busy schedule she still made time to read, whether it was a whole book or a single page. My mom took time in the day to nurture her inner self. She would read the Bible, and life for her was about her family; she didn't try to impress people; she just did her. Mom lived out the Bible passage about being content with what we had and didn't worry about what other people were doing. Competing for the valuable and visible items was not my mom's cup of tea.

My mother represents unconditional love and care. Whenever I was having a dark, cloudy moment, I could always go to my mom for guidance. She has experienced more of the things that I go through or will go through in the future; my mom knows what to say to put me in a better mood. For me, my mother's words spell reassurance and security. My mom is someone who inspires and represents love, safety, trust, and concern. Even though we have our disagreements, we don't let that affect our mother-daughter relationship. I will always love my mom no matter what.

Her advice and actions that projects her love and concern for me always find their way into my heart and mind. Even though I try to ignore it, it seems like my mom's opinion is all I could think about. The love my mother gives is infinite, eminent and limitless. Her love for my brother and me lives on beyond a human's life span.

My mom is the best creation that God has made. She has many amazing powers, like being able to multitask without any complaints. She cares for everyone no matter what without any demands. All mothers are wonderful in their own way. My mom is very special because she carried two children and can carry hardships, but she holds happiness, joy, and love. She smiles even though she might want to scream. My mom sings when she might want to cry. She cries when she's happy and laughs when she's nervous. My mom fights for what she believes in and does not take no for an answer when there is a way to solve the problem. My mom goes without, so her children can have. My mom loves unconditionally, and I love her just as much. She cries when her children excel and cheers really loudly when we get awards and make her proud. My mom is strong, and there is no other strength like hers. Her hugs and kisses can heal a broken heart. There are many wonderful moms that come in all different shapes, sizes, and colors, but no other mother can compare to mine! My mom did more than just give birth to me and my brother; she gave us joy, hope, and love.

I thank God for my mom, Mercer McClinton; she has taught me many things throughout the years. My mom is a wonderful woman, and I am proud to say I'm her daughter. My mom has taught me the importance of having a relationship with God and with Him anything is possible. There isn't anything more important for a mother to teach her children than to teach them how to have a relationship with God. Mom taught me how to endure and to never give up, even if I am having a hard time. Growing up, we endured some hard times, but through my mom's example of endurance, we learned to keep going, even in the hard times.

My mom never complains; she just learned to endure. If we will obey God and endure hardship like a good soldier (2 Timothy 2:3), there will be ample reward. My mom has taught my brother and me to be faithful to our words and to be faithful to God and His Word. My mom taught me the difference between right and wrong and taught me to make proper decisions.

I am here today as a result of my mother's faith. She believed that by teaching me all that she taught, she would never have to shed tears over a disobedient daughter. No, I haven't done everything right. Yes, I've messed up at times, and I've done some things in the past that I shouldn't have done. But God is forgiving, and the words of my mom always came to me in my time of need. God has been faithful to answer the prayers we prayed over the years.

Out of all the women and mothers in the world, there is no other that could take the place of my mom. Even though we get on each other's nerves at times, we still have unconditional love for one another. I know my mom loves me and cares for me. My mom loves me enough to ask where I'm going and what and with whom; she loves me enough to try and tell me to save my money for a rainy day; that's great because all children don't have parents that care for them the way mine cares for me.

There are so many things that I want to say to you Mom, I decided to put it in writing. In this story Mom, I want to share with you how I feel about all of the wonderful things that you have brought into my life. I want you to know how you have influenced my life and how you molded me and shaped me to be the woman I am now. You deserve to be honored; you deserve to be thanked.

When you became a mother, not once, but twice, you chose a life of selflessness. You chose a life of dedication, giving and caring. You chose to give up a life as an independent woman in exchange for a life of nurturing your kids. You made a decision that you have held strong to for a lifetime. You chose to give up all selfish thoughts and desires that we humans have in exchange for loving, caring and doing for both of your children. God blessed you with two wonderful children, a boy and a beautiful girl. You had a need inside of you to care for us and do for us unlike any mother I have ever seen. I know that I haven't always understood your point of view or agreed with all of your decisions. In some cases, I've probably been mad at you. It took me some time to get it. I had to be a woman I suppose, before I really understood, because as I child we just do not have the knowledge to comprehend the devotion and the commitment that mothers offer. I really appreciate everything you have done for me, and I am glad that you're my mom.

You could have chosen to be childless. You could have chosen a career and status. You could have chosen so many things for your path in life, but you chose us; you chose one boy, one girl and a bad dog we call Oreo. I want to thank you for being my mom and thank you for choosing me instead of something or someone else.

A mother does so many things for her child during a life's time. It would be utterly impossible to list them all. I can share things with you that I can share with no other. I don't have to worry about the repercussions. I don't have to worry about being judged. I just share with you my fears, my thoughts, my hopes and my dreams. I can share with you anything and everything that I have a need to share. When I'm feeling somewhat inadequate, you are right there to encourage me. You reassure me that there is nothing I can't do. You believed in me when I didn't even believe in myself. You gave me strength and courage. You taught me not to let fear of a challenge or fear of the unknown keep me from going after my dreams.

For a woman to have so little of the finer things in life and to do what you have done for others for an entire lifetime is commendable. No, you are not Mother Teresa, as the world knows her, but you are my Mother Teresa. You have done for your children and your grandchildren without hesitation, over and over again, for your entire life. I don't think you will ever get the appreciation and gratitude that you so deserve. You have repeatedly done without things that you need or desire in order to give what you have to your children. You have given way more than should ever be expected from one person.

I wonder if others are aware, as I am, of everything you've done for them. I know that if I needed a dollar you would hand it to me. You would give me your last dollar without any hesitation, without a question about why I might need it or how I was going to use it. You would just give to me your very last dollar. My mother's love is unconditional, and I love my mom unconditionally no matter what.

I am who I am because of you. I love you, and I thank you for everything you have done for me. I thank you for teaching me all that you can; I thank you for being there for me and raising me the best way you know how. I am very proud to say you are my mom, and I'd yell it to the entire world. Thank you, Mom, for just being you! I respect you and admire you. I am proud to be your daughter.

I've never known anyone in my life as giving as you. I look up to you, I appreciate you, and I am grateful for you. I accept you for who you are and who you are not. It makes me happy when I can do for you. I love you very very much, and I thank you for everything you have done for me and my brother. You are the best mom, and I wish everyone else could have a mom as great as you are.

A Mother's Heart

Dr. Cassundra White-Elliott

Mom- Gentle Strength

The Mildred Mae (Dunlap) Williams Story
by
Julia Lary

The Williams' Family Matriarch

A Mother's Heart

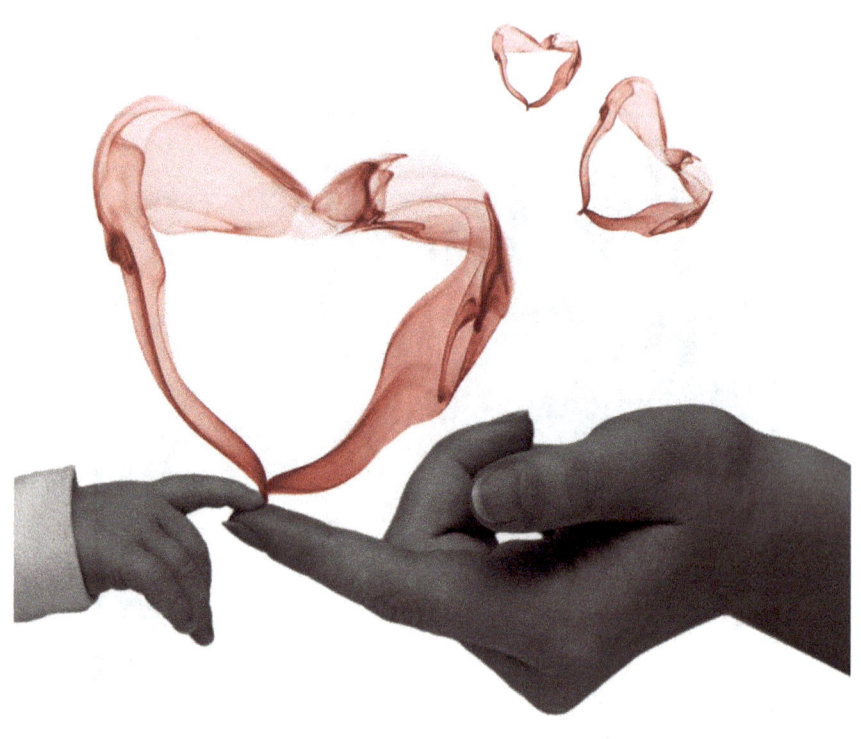

When you become of age, it's hard to look back on your life as a child. When I was about eleven years old, my dad left us to go to another city to find work in order to care for his family. My mom told us Dad would not be coming back until the weekend. Since there were many of us sharing a bed, I asked if I could sleep with her and the baby until his return. She said, "Yes."

I don't remember how many weeks or months Dad had been gone before the baby passed away, but I do know that I felt maybe I had gotten on the baby some way, somehow and killed her. My mom tried to convince me it was not my fault, but I felt Dad would say, "If you had not been in the bed with her, she would still be alive."

My mom showed me the doctor's report which read "SIDS." Did I know what that meant? Definitely not! SIDS is Sudden Infant Death Syndrome. Then, my mom said my baby sister didn't die because of me. She died of natural causes. Of course I asked when had she become sick, and Mom explained that we can sometimes get sick during the night, even as a healthy person, but no one will know what happened until the autopsy is complete. She told me she did not have to be sick to die. Later in life, I learned SIDS is also called "crib death." Bottom line, Dad didn't blame me, but seeing wreaths on doors afterwards always brought back the memories.

My dad's visits went from weekends to once a month to sporadic and finally not at all. Thankfully, there were friends and family members who were willing to help out because when the visits stopped so did the money for bills, etc. The only problem with this story was that the friends and family members who were willing to help didn't offer to give Mom money or food; they named a specific child from the family that they would take and care for. I didn't understand why we needed to leave home in order to receive help, but because of my mom's need for help, she agreed. I went to live with my dad's sister who wanted kids but was not able to have her own. The fifth child went to live with a church member, and the seventh child went to live with friends of the landlords who also had no children of their own.

Did I mention I was the second oldest of nine children? There were seven children when Dad left to go find work and by the time he decided to never return, there were nine. With that in mind, Mom still had to take care of six children. She became a welfare recipient but still needed to find work. She began working in a chicken house where chickens where prepared (killed and de-feathered, etc.) before making their way to the markets. She also worked for the "elite" cleaning house, preparing meals, laundry and whatever else needed to be done. There were also members of the "elite" who would let her pick up laundry, bring it home, wash and iron and deliver it back as a part-time job.

My mother was a strong woman, and one who never seemed to get tired, though I knew she did. On a side note, before I left home, I was the mother of all the other children, who had to make sure everyone was up in the mornings, dressed and ready for school, and we all had chores to do after school.

Mom was a sincere teacher of whatever she knew, and it appeared that since there was no dad in the home throughout most of our lives, she had the responsibility of teaching us everything. After having worked for a few years and realizing how hard it was to make ends meet, she instilled in us the value of work and working; that it was a requirement as well as a privilege, and we are to put all we have into any job we take on if we ever plan to succeed in life.

There were a couple of things she taught us that I've lived by each day of my life... 1) for every dollar you make always save a dime, and 2) never leave home without a wooden nickel (.05) for a phone call should an emergency arise. My mom taught us to never fall short of learning, always take the time to learn some things for ourselves because everything is not taught in classrooms, and it was not possible for her to remember everything we needed to know. She also stated that some of life experiences may never come up while we're home or still children, but as adults, we could still come to her and she would try to help find the answer. She used to say there were so many things of this world she could never teach us or help us with, but God can …. just ask Him. If you don't know what something means or how to perform a certain task, seek help. No question is a dumb question if you don't have the answer. If you don't know how to apply for credit or a job, ask someone who knows, read a book, or ask for wisdom from God. God can teach you all you need to know. I'm just a tool God uses to get you started. The rest is up to you and God.

Mom lived a life of brokenness for many years due to my father's separation from the family. I always knew that when she started talking about anger and prayer, she was either missing my dad or remembering how he left the family. I never knew the name of the song she'd always sing, but there's one verse I'll never forget … "happy am I when all the dark clouds roll away." She would also continually repeat the 23rd Psalms, which is how I learned the passage.

(*The Lord is my shepherd; I shall not want. He maketh me to lie down in green pastures; He leadeth me beside the still waters, He restoreth my soul; He leadeth me in the paths of righteousness for his name's sake. Yea, though I walk through the valley of the shadow of death, I will fear no evil; for thou art with me; Thy rod and thy staff they comfort me. Thou preparest a table before me in the presence of mine enemies; Thou anointest my head with oil; my cup runneth over, surely goodness and mercy shall follow me all the days of my life; and I will dwell in the house of the Lord forever*).

I didn't understand what it meant, but in church as a teenager, I was happy to announce that I knew the 23rd Psalms when asked if anyone could recite it verbatim. Before my dad left the family, we would always pray the Lord's Prayer when we were told to pray because in our early training to pray, that is what we were taught by our parents and the teaching of the church. In later years, Mom told us the bible says, "Ask and it shall be given to you," meaning when you pray, ask for whatever it is that you're in need of, and He will give it to you. At that moment, she explained that prayer to the Lord can be done in other ways, such as talking to God just as we talk to her. Mom said prayer is the channel by which we receive our blessings.

Other times, I knew Mom was still dealing with her brokenness when she began to teach us about forgiveness. Forgiveness frees both parties involved. Mom stressed to us that we will have broken hearts even among us siblings, so it's very important that she teach us forgiveness. She indicated that once we become adults and have our own children, it is important to teach them God's word, teach them to read the bible every chance they get, and most importantly, we must teach our children how to forgive as well. If our children are ever exposed to our anger, make sure they're around when we show grace. They must know that God's grace is sufficient for all… His mercy is new every morning. She said, "I am telling you this because I want you to learn from the mistakes of your parents, so that you won't have to go through the same thing I did and pass it on to your children." She added, "The bible says in Ephesians 4: 26… do not let the sun go down while you're still angry, and do not give the devil a foothold." That means, forgive when you are hurt and don't take your resentments/anger to bed. Forgiveness positions you where God can bless you.

My mom was an excellent soprano singer. We were taught to sing by my parents who could sing well in my opinion. We were raised in the church and thus have attended church all our lives. As a song leader in the church, my mom and dad would teach us songs on Saturdays that they were planning to sing on Sunday. Although we did not own a piano, my parents learned music the old fashioned way, through Solfege or as some know it ... solfa syllables (do, re, mi, fa, sol, la, ti, do). My first solo was taught to me at age ten by my mom ... "How Firm a Foundation." Here are the words to the beautiful song loved by my mom:

"How firm a foundation, ye saints of the Lord, is laid for your faith in His excellent word! What more can He say than to you He hath said, to you who for refuge to Jesus have fled,

Fear not, I am with thee; O be not dismayed, For I am thy God, and will still give thee aid; I'll strengthen thee, help thee, and cause thee to stand, upheld by My righteous, omnipotent hand.

When through the deep waters I call thee to go, the rivers of woe shall not thee overflow; For I will be with thee thy troubles to bless, and sanctify to thee thy deepest distress.

When through fiery trials thy pathways shall lie, My grace, all sufficient, shall be thy supply; The flame shall not hurt thee; I only design thy dross to consume and thy gold to refine.

The soul that on Jesus still leans for repose, I will not, I will not desert to his foes; that soul, though all hell should endeavor to shake, I'll never, no never, no never forsake!"

After many years of singing the song, I really didn't understand what it meant or what my mom was trying to say when she taught the song to me, except I felt she was still dealing with her brokenness. I believe now, God was saying to her... *"Fear not, for I have redeemed you, I have summoned you by name, you are mine. When you pass through the waters, I will be with you; and when you pass through the rivers, they will not sweep over you. When you walk through the fire, you will not be burned; the flames will not set you ablaze. I am the Lord, your God, the Holy One of Israel, your Savior"* (Isaiah 43: 1-3).

Even though my mom only finished ninth grade, she was very cognizant. She was a brilliant learner in her efforts to improve herself. She was not afraid to tackle any task no matter how large or small. Mom read the Bible frequently and knew as much as anyone I've known of its contents. As adults, we teased her about not being afraid to jump in with the "well to do" church goers, and she would say, "My bible tells me no one is more than I am, that we are all equal in God's eyes, but I'm to put others before me in that I'm not to be selfish as in thinking of myself first." (Paraphrased)

I admired my mom for her tenacity. She was strong willed and the most giving person I've known. She was full of love; with nine children, she definitely had enough to share. She loved us all equally, and regardless of our faults, she always tried to direct us down the right path as much as she was able, and as she would say, "I'll leave the rest to God." The thing I'd hoped would be different after a few years was to see my mom and dad reunited before we became adults. At fifteen years of age, I had my own car and visited my mom and siblings often.

As young adults, my siblings and I showed our appreciation to Mom by helping her as much as possible, by purchasing TVs, small appliances, clothing or whatever she needed up to and including a car. She was a one-of-a-kind mom who went to be with Jesus in 1996, on Easter Sunday. What a wonderful celebration it was with all the children there. God blessed her with a good life before her departure. Her love still shines in all of us today. Even the grandkids who knew her speak of the legacy of love she left behind.

Dr. Cassundra White-Elliott

Mother of Strength and Love

by
Maria Guzman

A Mother's Heart

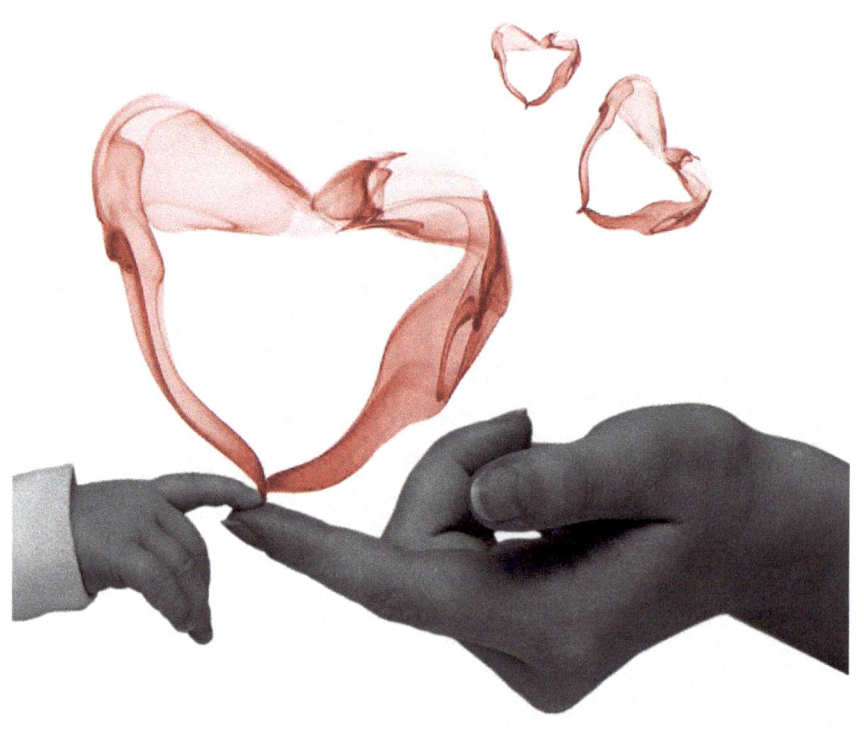

My mother represents strength and love. A woman, who was anxious to learn and experiment with life, decided to travel to the U.S., leaving behind her family and relatives. My mother was born and raised in Mexico City. She married at a very young age, only to get divorced a year later because her husband at that time was not capable of accepting and supporting my mother after having lost their first born child. My mother continued with her life, trying to reestablish herself, after a major loss in her life. Soon, she met my father, remarried, and had four children. However, as the years passed, my parents were divorced and all contact was lost with my father.

Carmen is her name, and she is strength and love. My mother has endured and struggled with life as a single parent. Mother worked hard to provide for her children and often came home tired. However, Carmen continued with life, making sure her family was safe. She enrolled into night school, while working full time during the day. Within a year, Mother graduated and completed her internship hours to become a hair dresser. The funny part of this is that my siblings, including myself were used as models for haircuts, hair perms, coloring, or bleaching hair. My mother had a way to convince us of her crazy hairdo projects.

My mother is a strong woman, who taught us to be independent and to love. My mother's favorite quote that she often repeated is, "Learn from the past, live the present moment, and work for the future" (Unknown Author). My mother made sure we ate a warm meal, and she stayed up late at night for her daughters to get home. She often talks to us about keeping our eyes open for those who want to cause harm or any problems. Although my mother was very independent, she had a very traditional way of thinking. She often talked to her daughters about keeping their virginity and dressing appropriately. However, mother did not turn her back on her children even when one of her children advised her of being gay, or another daughter losing her virginity before getting married, and having another daughter who was a single mother.

    My mother represents strength and love. Although my mother does not have a higher education, she is wise and did the best she could have for her family. Today, my mother is happy and still single. She never remarried and enjoys her time with her grandchildren. She enjoys going to church, participating in the community events, and volunteers her time in non-profit agencies. My mother is the best, and I'm glad she made the choice of reestablishing herself here in the U.S. because otherwise my life and my siblings' lives would have been a totally different story.

Life of Inspiration

Tyler Kowalski-Foley & Haley Keil

A Mother's Heart

Motherhood is defined by many aphorisms
Mothers' virtues shine through like light through a prism
Danielle's values burst through on a level of elevation
That is why she leads a life of inspiration

Homemaker

Danielle Foley is a homemaker, and this is one of the most important jobs that a person can have. She chooses to stay home most of the week and invests in her family's lives. Consequently, her children have received an above average education through her tireless efforts to homeschool. Furthermore, her loving touch is always seen in the house. The house is clean, the laundry is washed, and homemade meals are always ready. Staying at home has helped her invest in her children's lives more than most people ever have the time to do. All her children have experienced helping her cook and clean. Everyone helps out and must learn to be responsible. Her children have cultivated life skills and responsibility that will serve them for the rest of their lives.

Patience

Danielle is one of the most patient people ever to be encountered. To begin, she watches two year olds at church. Many people dread this difficult age, and they would never volunteer to be in a room full of two year olds for several hours, but Danielle welcomes the children with an open heart. She says that this age is her favorite because the children are learning and growing. Instead of focusing on the tantrums and behavioral learning curves, Danielle focuses on the immense progress she sees within the children.

Danielle also homeschooled her three children. They have moved in and out of public school and homeschool, but for a few years, she had all three children at home with her. That took patience. She needed to watch over, plan for, and help out all three on their different homework for their grade level. She did it all happily and went above and beyond to enroll her kids in Bible studies, youth groups, Boy Scouts of America, and additional extracurricular activities. As a result, her children are happy, studious, and involved in the community.

Leadership

Danielle is a leader in many ways. First off, most obviously, she is a mom. She is involved in her children's lives and leads by example. She does not tell her children how to behave and then refuse to model the behavior. If she tells one of her sons to take care of his elders, then she will do the same for the people in her life. In this way, she has instilled invaluable wisdom, morals, and priorities in her children. Her children, in turn, live their lives differently than their peers do. Her children are respectful, merciful, and hardworking; they live their lives to praise God.

Additionally, Danielle holds a leadership position at a ministry called Community Bible Study. Danielle has proven her dedication to this ministry for many years, and now she has the opportunity to guide others in their quest to live their lives in Jesus' image. Once again, Danielle leads by example. If she tells her peers to study the lessons every day, then she will do that same. She also does not lead blindly. Danielle does her homework and takes initiative by deeply studying the Bible daily and attending leadership seminars whenever she can. Danielle was also the treasurer for her boys' troop in Boy Scouts of America.

Danielle is also active at her children's dance studio. She works at the front desk and helps backstage during performances. These tasks may seem menial, but Danielle brings her work ethic and her passion for helping others wherever she goes; consequently, she empowers the people around her, and she helps all the day-to-day work run a little bit smoother. As a result, she is respected and admired. In live theater, there are always emergencies and unforeseen hurdles, and Danielle has helped solve many of these issues.

Sacrifice and Humility

Danielle works around the clock to ensure her family is cared for and happy. When she could be relaxing or pursuing her own interests, she is helping the people around her pursue what is important to them. Danielle does not have to work at the dance studio, lead at Community Bible Study, homeschool her children, or watch ten two year olds on a Sunday morning - but she does. She happily blesses the people around her without thinking of herself; she is the definition of altruism. For instance, her two oldest children decided that they wanted to attend a public high school. Danielle loves homeschooling, so the choice was difficult. Nevertheless, she put their needs in front of her own and both her boys are happy with the education they received. She made all the educational opportunities available to them - even if she was happy with the situation they had at that moment.

Danielle is humble: she does not make a point to talk about herself or her achievements. Instead, she focuses on encouraging other people. When she is complimented, she gracefully accepts it and then returns the favor immediately. She does not serve her family, the kids at church, and the people in the community for the praise and recognition. Contrarily, many of the tasks that she does every day remain thankless, and she is perfectly satisfied with the happiness she sees on the other people's faces. She has a true, rare servant's heart. Whether or not people take the time to thank her, everyone notices her hard work, and everyone is grateful for her. She is appreciated and admired.

Lighthearted and Loving

Danielle always finds the good in every situation, but she still finds a way to be empathetic and recognize the weight of the situation. If you have a bad day, she will be there to listen and acknowledge how you feel, but she will also point out the good in the midst of all the bad. Danielle genuinely has a happy disposition; her laugh is bright and readily available. Just being in her presence lifts people's spirits. She is humorous and always ready to converse and connect with other people.

Danielle is also incredibly loving. Despite hard times that come with raising children, she continues to love on her children and respond - not react - to the difficult situations that arise. Although she may feel frustrated at times, she is a seemingly infinite river of grace. If someone in her household makes a mistake, there are rightful consequences, but she still shows mercy and forgives over and over again. These characteristics carry over into all her other interpersonal interactions. Everything is governed by gentleness. If she disagrees with a person's opinion, she respectfully voices what she feels. If she feels the need to correct someone, she never scolds. Instead, she gently and firmly suggests what needs to be done. One of the most beautiful aspects about her is how she treats children. Many people hastily and roughly correct children, and they never allow the child to have an input in what is going on, but Danielle approaches everyone with respect. She accomplishes what needs to be done, but she is loving and respectful while she does it. She does not impose on the child in an authoritative manner. The way that people treat those who are under their authority tells a lot about the person. Danielle treats everyone, even the little two year olds, with uncommon respect and courtesy.

Determination and Faith

Perhaps the most inspiring out of all these traits is Danielle's determination. When she was in the middle of working on her Bachelor's degree, she was blessed with her first son. Then, she was torn between having the traditional college experience and being a fulltime mother to her new little boy. Danielle had faith that God would give her strength, and she sacrificed an enormous amount of her time to be involved in her son's early years. Many people can't muster up the strength to finish a degree under normal circumstances, but Danielle finished her degree in Biology - a notoriously difficult major - with a young child. She showed uncommon determination and faith.

Later on in her life, Danielle suffered through a nearly fatal bout of bone cancer. She stayed incredibly strong and had incredible faith in the Lord. Her family prayed and prayed, and eventually, the Lord healed her body. After she recovered, over the next few years, her family of three grew to a family of five when Jordan and Annaliza were born. She has remained strong throughout her entire life, and now, she pours her strength into caring for her family. Her faith and determination are huge parts of her character and they influence everyone around her for the better.

All in all, Danielle Foley inspires more people than she ever realizes. Her choice to be a homemaker, and her patience, leadership, sacrifice, humility, lightheartedness, love, determination, and faith inspires everyone around her. Thank you for being who you are and contributing in so many people's lives!

About the Authors

Tyler Kowalski-Foley is a nineteen-year-old student at Grand Canyon University where he is studying Computer Science. Tyler is an Eagle Scout, and he is currently taking steps to join the Air National Guard. Tyler enjoys hiking, playing video games, and studying math theories. Tyler is passionate about community service and is very involved in his Christian faith.

Haley Keil is an eighteen-year-old student at College of the Desert. She will be graduating this summer with an Associate's degree in Psychology and attending Grand Canyon University in Fall 2017. There, she will pursue a Bachelor's in English. Haley enjoys dancing, drawing, hiking, and being involved at church. She looks forward to a career filled with writing creatively and professionally.

A Caring Soul

by
Fernando Lescano

To my dear children, If I had to choose between loving you and breathing, I would use my last breath to tell you, "I Love You."
- Anonymous

A Mother's Heart

There will always be that one person who will always care for you no matter what you may do to him/her. In his/her eyes, you can do no wrong, and he/she will forever be proud of you no matter how small of a thing you succeed in. To me that person is my mother. She is the strongest woman I know. Thanks to her influence in my life, it has made me the person I am today. My mother has been there my entire life and has done everything possible for me to have a better life than she did. For that, I will always be grateful and hold her sacrifices near and dear to my heart.

My mother always wanted me to succeed in everything I set my mind to. She always would ask me, "Wonderful son, how do you plan on doing that?" or "Have you planned this out right?" and "Won't it interfere with what you already have going on? Otherwise, if it's possible, you can set it aside for a later time?" After I laid out all my plans and they met her requirements, she would always end with, "Okay perfect, son. How can I help you?" Once I heard those words, I knew I had her approval and support.

My mother is the most important person in my life and will forever be my biggest support and hero in my life because she has been like a mother and a father to me. She is kind, loving, and nurturing but has also been very stern and firm in her rules. She has pushed me to do better than what I have done and in a sense shaped the person I have become. For my mother, the idea of not being able to do something didn't apply. To her, there is always a solution. We just have to figure it out, and we may not like the solution or the work it will take to get to that solution, but nonetheless, there will always be one.

My mother comes from a background of people that are notorious for their old sayings, and my mother is no exception. In fact, I love that about her, and over time, I grew to use them myself, and they push me to do live up to those old sayings. Her most used sayings have always been, "Do your best, and it will show in your work. And, if you feel the burden of your work on shoulders, use your backbone to strengthen your core and continue forward." These words have always been open to interpretation, and the beauty is my mother would speak these words and would not explain them but just say them without thinking. These words have pushed me to achieve everything up to this point in my life, and I believe I will carry them until the day I pass.

Looking back to my childhood, I always wondered what made my mom the way she is, such a brave, humble, and caring person, with the drive to push our family forward, especially when my father lacked in his role in our family, even well after he succumbed to his own affairs and left our world forever, leaving behind his debt and a broken home struggling to stay together and survive. Resentment grew in my heart for my father, but my mother would always say, "He was your father, and although he left us all with a sour taste in our mouth, we must not judge others for their shortcomings. You cannot deny that he never let us starve or live on the streets. He provided for us in the best way he could. The rest is his lament." I just sat there and could not believe how sincere my mother was in regards to my father's memory. Again, I questioned where that all could have originated from. How could my mom just pick herself up and continue on with such determination and still humble herself, even after all father had done to our family. I began to wonder if I would understand the reason how mother grew to be the person she is today.

I remember one spring afternoon when I was helping my grandmother move things around her small home and clean up and organize all her things as I did every spring when I would visit her in Mexico. I came across a small box that I had never seen before. It was covered in colorful ribbons glued with cornstarch. I held it up and asked aloud, "Grandma, what's this little box here? I've never seen it before." My grandma just waved me to bring it closer, and when she had it in clear focus in front of her, she replied, "It's your mother's box of things. Your grandfather found it tucked away in between the clay shingles of the front porch while he was replacing them last October. I honestly haven't had a chance to look at it. What do you say we look into your mother's past shall we?" I nodded in agreement with excitement. As I opened it, I asked aloud, "How do you know it is my mom's?" My grandmother said, "I remember every ribbon your mother ever wore in her hair, and they are all decorating this little paper box." With those last words, the box was opened, and inside I found a stack of old photos that were old and worn along with a couple of rolls of photo negatives. I started looking through them with my grandmother and what we were about to find still to this day brings tears to my eyes.

The first photograph was my mother and her friends in cheerleading outfits, and she had the biggest smile I had ever seen on her. The next was my mother in a really pretty turquoise silk dress trimmed with white lace and embellished with pearl like beads and right behind her were six outfits all displayed on mannequins. The next photograph was of her with an old-fashioned singer sewing machine. The next one was of her in an old patchy dress. Her hair was up in a braid, she had no shoes on, and she was in front of a floor level mud sculpted stove. Her face was bright red from the heat of the sun and fire of the burning firewood.

In the following photo, she was pulling the weeds from between the tall cornstalks in the fields. Her cheeks and bare shoulders had fine slices with faint blood streaks. Each photo made me feel as though I was looking through time and seeing what my mother's life was like. I turned and saw my grandmother in tears, and she found herself saying, "The day your mother left, a piece of me fell apart. She was the one who helped me the most around this house. She was the first one up and the last one to lie down. She never once protested or pouted about her chores. She simply went on with her chores and encouraged everybody to keep up the pace. She helped your grandfather in the field, would cook and feed everybody, helped carry firewood home, and would still come home and help me braid fine palm braids that were up to twenty yards in length. When she left, all I did was cry. I resented your grandfather for making her choose between marriage or leaving to the states. I couldn't sleep or eat when you mother left. The very thought of your mother crossing that border and all odds against her was way more than I could bear," she said with tears running down her face. "I felt as though I would never see her again."

The time came when I had to return home to California. I remember one afternoon while my mom and I were folding laundry, I turned and asked my mother, "Mom, you know you hardly talk about your life in Mexico before you came to the states." She then paused for a second and then continued to fold and said, "Well, son. What do you want to know?" Naturally, I responded, "Well everything." She chuckled and went on by saying, "Well, that's a broad statement." I said, "Yeah, true. Okay well, tell me the highlights." She went on to say, "Okay well, let's see. I was raised on a farm and went to school up to the second grade, but there was not enough money for me continue to attend, so I stopped going to school and started to work instead. "Work?" I questioned. "But, you were in the second grade when you stopped. You would have only been seven years old." My mother paused again and said in a low voice, "I was twelve actually. School was a bit expensive and not to mention an extra cost. And in reality, men were more of a priority to attend because they would be the breadwinners." I stood there in disbelief of what my mother had just spoken, but I went on to ask, "Well, did you ever go back to school?"

My mom looked down and stayed quiet for what seemed like forever and then said, "Yes, by the time I turned seventeen, they had adult skills classes that were available to the community, and there was a sewing course for all those who wished to attend. I took it right away, but unfortunately, it became to be a bit expensive even though the course was free. We still needed to provide our own materials and equipment. After a while, I just couldn't afford it, so I had to stop going, but I did enjoy it and from what I did learn, it helped me make a lot of different outfits that lasted me for a long time. I even got to wear a dress I made for my civil marriage ceremony. I was filled with such hope, and I was crushed the day I had to pack up my things and clean up my station. I resumed my old duties around the house, and your grandparents were glad to have me home. My father even went on to say, 'This is where you belong in the fields and your place is in a kitchen. Don't you forget that.'

She continued by saying, "A year passed by, and I noticed the ugly butcher's son always being extra nice to your grandfather and asking about me. He would always end the conversation with, 'I tell you, sir, if she would be my wife, she would want for nothing.' Your grandfather would just nod and say, 'You're too kind, son. I'll have to pass along those good intentions on to my daughter.' Till one day the butcher and that big-lipped idiot came knocking on my door wishing to talk to my parents. The next thing I knew, they are asking to marry me off with that idiot. Nope! Not a chance in hell was I going to do that. I had somebody I was already talking to, and to be frank, your grandparents didn't agree because he was in a higher social class than me, but we didn't care about that. All we cared was for each other, and I wasn't going to live a miserable life being the wife of a butcher. Then, your grandfather tried to talk to me into it, but there was no way I was even considering to marry that big-lipped fool. With not another word, he yelled, 'You marry that boy, or you leave to live with your brothers in the states and work out there for the family! Make your choice! Either way you're packing your things young lady! Do I make myself clear?' He walked off in his usual furry. I sat there with tears in my eyes with such disbelief. I couldn't believe what was happening. I wasn't going to marry a man I found repulsive, but I also didn't want to leave everything I knew behind, especially my mother, but I would rather die than to live that life, so I was forced to leave even though it killed me.

"The day came when I had to leave, and I felt like my whole world was ending right before my eyes. I packed all my things and walked out my home for what seemed like the very last time. I left knowing it would be a very long time before I would see my home again. The very thought unsettled my very core. I walked up to my parents to say goodbye, but my father walked away and said, 'Hurry up! You're going to miss your bus, and I'm not paying for another bus ticket. She continued, "My poor mother looked as though she was going to fall to her knees from the pain of having to say goodbye. Tears ran down her face, and I found myself crying on her shoulder saying, 'I don't want to go, Mother. This is so horrible! Please, talk to dad. It's not too late.' She said, 'The answer is simple, sweetie. Marry that nice young man, and you can stay to become a wife and a mother yourself. It's the only way.' I whispered, 'I'm sorry, Mother, but I can't.' She then hugged and held me saying, 'My beautiful girl, don't forget where you come from. Remember, I will always love you and I'll pray for your safety wherever you are. I left with a deep sorrow in my heart and a radiating fear in my soul as the bus drove off getting me closer to what I had only heard was a terrifyingly dangerous and agonizingly painful crossing of the border. My stomach went into knots at the thought of what awaited me in just two days' time.

The crossing was horrible. It was more than anything I ever imagined. During the first attempt, I met a little twelve-year-old girl. She was on her way to meet up with her mother in Texas, who had left her in the care of her grandmother when she was only two years old, to go the states in order to provide for them both. The time had come when her mother had made enough money to send for her to come and be with her. Her story brought tears of joy to my eyes for her. The guides were weird men, who stunk of liquor and weed and would take all kinds of drugs that made them crazy and crude. One in particular kept eyeing the little girl and made her feel uncomfortable. The first day went by. We traveled on foot, and the little girl was exhausted and clung onto my arm. I kept encouraging her to keep going, saying it was almost over and she would see her mom soon. The night came, and we all slept next to each other in that freezing desert. I remember telling her the next day was the day she would have to give it her all. After saying that, I drifted into a deep sleep."

"The next morning, the guides kicked us awake, telling us to get moving quickly, but the little girl was nowhere to be found. I looked all over in hopes to see her scared somewhere reaching out for my hands, but she was gone. I told the guide, 'Please, there's somebody missing.' He slapped me straight across my face and yelled, 'Get moving!' He looked at me with an evil smirk, and at that moment, I knew she was gone and there was nothing I could do but cry. Your uncle held me and told me to keep moving and not make a scene. To this day, I still picture that poor child like it was just yesterday, looking at me scared and tired, telling me how she wants her mom, while holding me with her small little hands."

A Mother's Heart

My mother paused and held her stomach as though she was going to be sick, and she said in a soft tone, "Only God knows what that monster did to that poor defenseless innocent child. I held my mom to calm her down, instantly regretting having her relive such a traumatic experience. At that moment, I knew why she had avoided that conversation. The very memory was enough to even make the strongest man cry. I couldn't believe what she had gone through. She continued to say, "I would get caught that night and spend the night in a cold cell for two days and released back into Tijuana. I would try three more times before actually crossing that cursed border. The second time, a man was found dead in the morning from a snakebite in his sleep. The third time, your uncle was ganged up by the guides, trying to protect my innocence, and we were left out there in the desert by those monsters. For two days, we stayed in the same place until border patrol found us. The fourth and final time, a woman who was carrying her newborn baby allowed herself to be abused by those monsters in order to have water for her baby's instant milk, but unfortunately, the baby overheated and died on the last day before crossing the border. She buried the poor child out there in the desert. I can still hear her silent sobs as her hands unearthed that hot desert sand to lay her baby to rest. The next day, we reached the border and waited to cross until it was dawn. The guide signaled us to run as fast as we could, jump the fence, and run into the van that was waiting for us on the other side. The signal was sent out, so I ran and I gave it all I had left until I finally made it. Your uncle followed shortly after and then the rest."

I stood there speechless, and all I could think was she endured all that just to come to the United States not knowing what would happen to her or she could expect to come across. In my eyes, she will always be my hero. She has always been such a strong woman, and she has shaped me into the person I am today. I had always wondered what the reason was for my mother's drive and why she was such a determined woman. I never again had to question why my amazing mother was the way she is today. She is my rock and will forever be the most important person in my life. She has earned my respect and love. I don't know what I would do without her in my life.

A Mother's Heart

Dr. Cassundra White-Elliott

A Letter to My Mother

by
Elaine M. Tolentino

A Mother's Heart

Dearest Mama,

My nuptials and the birth of my son were the most fulfilling and exciting events in my life. Another event is not precisely a positive one at first glance, but it is one of the motives I am writing to you today. Recently, you faced a parent's worst nightmare when your son Melver passed away. Our lives were no longer as we had known it, and the agony was visible like a broken bone that aches when it is cold.

In the early days of his passing, I watched you get up, get dressed, prepare meals for the guests and sit beside his coffin. You had the thousand-yard stare, looking and focusing on nothing. Your eyes were numb. Yet, you were strong enough to carry out the plan of the day. I cannot begin to imagine how you felt. Not every child loves his/her mother, but every mother loves her child. You have grieved the too-soon, startling, violent end of your faiths and ideas without a chance to say good-bye. You stood over the patch of dirt that shelters the buried body of your son. I am sure you wondered, "How can this be happening to us?"

Over the previous months, I understand that the time I spent with the family members has become almost nonexistent. These days, I have been dealing with my grief on my own. I am willing to say I believe I am better than most in handling our lost because of my faith. I owe that to you. You taught me to offer my life to the Lord and to lay my worries before Him. I live in the confirming and filling promise that the world I am living is not the only world there is. I hold on to the Word of God and hope in, trust on, and support the victory of Jesus Christ.

Your strength in the darkest time of our lives reveals the profundity of resiliency in the human spirit. I am immersed in my seat while writing this, and I have tears in my eyes, as I recollect the trauma and despair of losing my brother. We all believe he was doing the right thing: exposing corruption and making a stand. His political rivals cut your son's life short. Despite the tragedy around us, you always gave a sense of hope, purpose and direction. Your ability to share your own journey inspires strength and courage.

As I lay next to your grandson Elijah every night, I cannot help but to hold him a little tighter each time because I am aware now that tomorrow, in this life, is not promised. I often wonder if you too wake up in the morning and think for a moment everything is just fine with the world and then your mind links with your eyes and you are reminded that he is gone. If so, how do you handle it? Mama, I am full of sentiments. I am only human. Some days, I get by, but some days are a little harder. I wish you were here all the time, so you can help guide my sister, Maila in her grieving process too. She's tough on the outside, but I know she hides her tears also. We understand our other brother, Jun, needs your presence more than us since he is dealing with the trauma worse than us because he was first at the scene when Melver was killed. We have always been independent throughout our adult lives. I know at times it seems we do not need you, but the certainty that you are there helps us sleep better at night. We are looking forward to your next visit here in the States.

Well, on a brighter side of this note- I have some good news to share with you. Being the youngest of your four children, the importance of higher education is something I took for granted in my younger years. You advised me many times to pursue a degree since I moved out of your house. I tackled many struggles in my personal and professional life because I did not listen to you. This year, I have dedicated the time and everything needed for academic success. My husband and I had made many sacrifices to allow me to focus on education, and I finally enrolled in school and now have a chance to gain a degree just like you always hoped for. I will try to apply the same meticulousness to my academic studies as you did while taking care of us. I believe I will embody you well through my years in college and beyond.

I might as well apologize here. In my teenage years, I know I was a tough cookie to handle. I made your life more stressful than it should have been. All the sass and backtalk was a mistake. I should have never treated you how I did. I had the impression that my life was difficult because you never gave in to my wants, but I failed to realize that you gave everything I needed. I want to apologize for all the hurt I have caused and all the pain I have put you through because you sure did not deserve it. Your tough love was what we needed; we did not grow up to be entitled adults. Instead, we work hard for whatever we want in life just like you. We are all successful in our own ways because you did not spoil us. I did not know any better, and for that, I am sorry.

Thank you, Mama, for all your patience towards us. Thank you for being a loving and caring grandma to my son. Thank you for molding me to the woman who I have become. You know I love you. If I don't say is as often as I should, I am sorry. I certainly hope that you feel it. Please take care of yourself too. I want you to know it is okay to show you are grieving. You cannot force your heart to disregard the pain it feels. But, I believe that every person grieves differently. One thing is for sure though, it changes us. So please continue to live each day for God. For us who carry the burden of grief, all we can do is acknowledge our daily struggle. Well, best close for now. Take care and God bless.

Always,
Elaine

A Mother's Heart

Dr. Cassundra White-Elliott

My Best Friend

by
Karen Ruiz

A best friend is someone who is there for you through the good and the bad. A best friend is someone who doesn't give up on you and motivates you to be the best version of yourself.

A Mother's Heart

Growing up, I had a lot of friends and acquaintances. Because of my personality, I wanted to be everyone's friend. I searched for a best friend in everyone, someone I could tell my deepest secrets and my biggest fears and laugh uncontrollably with. No matter what I tried, I never found that person. They either hurt me and took advantage of my kindness and judged me for how fragile I was when it came to certain situations. Whenever I was hurt and felt like I couldn't take it anymore, I would turn, and my mom would be right there with open arms, ready to love me and tell me everything was going to be okay and that God had bigger plans for me and to remind me that everything in this world was temporary and that I had to keep pushing forward. God was only preparing me for the biggest blessings of my life.

I thought that is what mothers were supposed to do, be there for their kids and give them words of encouragement. Soon, I came to find out that wasn't their duty. Going to a multicultural public high school and walking down the hallway, I heard all kinds of stories. I heard kids say their mom chose their boyfriends over them, and other moms were kicking out their sixteen year olds and abusing them. This was all obscure to me, and I paid no attention to it because my mom would never do such a thing.

All the times my mom would yell at me and hit me with the chankla was because she loved me and would do anything for me. All the times she wouldn't allow me to go to all the "cool" parties with the older crowd was because she loved me and wanted the best for me, not because she didn't want me to enjoy my childhood or teenage years. All the times I thought she was trying to embarrass me in front of my friends was her simply showing she loved me. Growing up, I always wanted the "cool" mom, the mom who would not care to check up on me when I was out or give me money to go out without having to earn it.

It wasn't until I got older when I realized so much. The whole time I was searching for a best friend in other kids who were completely lost as I was, my best friend was right there by my side this entire time. I was blindsided and didn't realize it. My mom, the woman who fought everything to not let me become another statistic and to not see me fall, the woman I call Mommy and showed me unconditional love was my best friend all along. She was the only one who stayed up with me all night helping me do all the crafty projects I was assigned and didn't do on time because I procrastinated. She never complained. Whenever I would cry, she was there to wipe my tears and to pinch me, so I would have a real reason to cry. All the nights she spent with me restless in a hospital simply because my body would give up on me time from time and she would make me my special foods without complaining. All the nights where I had bad dreams and felt lonely, her bed was the first bed I would crawl into. Yes, even at the age of nineteen, I still crawled into bed with my mommy because next to her is where I felt safe.

    I wish I realized that my mom was my best friend all along when I was younger. It would have saved me from so many heartaches and mistakes and cruel people.

    So, thank you, Mami! For everything you've done for me. For loving me even when I made it impossible to love me. For waiting for me at the end of the finish line with a smile on your face. For believing in me even when I didn't believe in myself. For reminding me that the best is yet to come and to focus on God because He is the only one who can help me spiritually and physically. For letting me crawl into bed with you in the middle of the night and taking all the blankets. Thank you for loving me in your own special way. It wasn't always with nice words, but it sure was with love. If I ever become half the woman you are, I know I have made it a long way. Words will never come close to express my love for you. Because of you, I am slowly but surely becoming the independent woman you raised me to be. I'm sorry if I haven't been the perfect daughter, but I can promise you that I'm trying to become the best version of myself every day because of you. Gracias por ser mi major amiga mami, Te Quiero Tanto, Tanto cada dia un poco mas.

Gift of Salvation for Non-Believers

"For all have sinned, and come short of the glory of God."
Romans 3:23

This section was written especially for non-believers, those who have not accepted the gift of salvation. The gift of salvation saves souls from eternal damnation and is a free gift offered by God himself. John 3:16-18 says, *"For God so loved the world, that he gave his only begotten Son, that whosoever believeth in him should not perish, but have everlasting life. For God sent not his Son into the world to condemn the world; but that the world through him might be saved. He that believeth on him is not condemned: but he that believeth not is condemned already, because he hath not believed in the name of the only begotten Son of God."* This section of scripture tells us God's purpose for giving His son Jesus to the world. The world was in a bad condition. The world was overwrought with sin; the people were living for fleshly desires rather than for God's desires.

As a result of the world's conditions, God decided that He would offer the perfect sacrifice that would save the world from being a place where people were lost and had no hope. He decided that His own son could stand in proxy for the sin-filled world, taking all sin upon Himself.

So Jesus came, born of a virgin, to save this dying world. He walked on this earth for 33 ½ years, doing the work of His Heavenly

Father. At the appointed time, He died by way of crucifixion upon a cross at Calvary, on Golgatha's hill. He shed his blood and died for you and for me. Because His blood was pure, it paid the penalty for all unrighteousness and gave those who believe in Him direct access to His father's throne.

Scripture tells us in Matthew 27:51 that the veil of the temple was ripped in two from top to bottom, at the moment that Jesus' spirit left His body. As a result of the veil's removal, we are no longer required to have a high priest make intercession for us. We, as the children of the Most High God, are able to approach the throne God for ourselves, and Jesus sits on the right hand of the Father making intercession for us.

But what is even more miraculous than God offering His own son as the perfect sacrifice was the fact that when Jesus was placed in grave clothes and placed in a tomb, He only remained there until the third day. God would not have it that His son would remain in the heart of the earth forever. In order for people to believe in the awesome power of God and His dear son Jesus, a miracle had to be performed. So, on the third day, after Jesus died on the cross, He was resurrected, demonstrating the omnipotence of God. This very act was the act that would cause people to believe in a god that reigns supreme and holds the power of the universe in His very hands, a god that could save them from themselves.

Today, if you are an unbeliever, you can change your destiny. You can change where you will spend your eternity. Our Heavenly Father gives us the freedom of choice about how we want to live our life here on earth and how we want to spend eternity. In Deuteronomy 30:19, God boldly declares, *"I call heaven and earth to record this day against you, that I have set before you life and death, blessing and cursing: therefore choose life, that both thou and thy seed may live."*

So, dear friend what choice will you make today? Will you spend your eternity with the Creator or will you suffer Hell's eternal flames? Again, the choice is yours. Just as the men aboard the ship who were with Jonah became believers, you too can make a choice to accept the only one and true living God as your god.

If after reading the above passages, you have decided that you want to spend your eternity in Heaven with God, the creator, and His son Jesus, and the Holy Spirit, read through what has affectionately come to be known as the Roman's Road. This is the road to salvation. As you read through the scriptures that comprise the Roman's Road, you will also read the explanation for each scripture so you will have clarity about what you are reading and confessing.

The Roman's Road to Salvation

The road to salvation begins with Romans 3:23 which declares, *"For all have sinned, and come short of the glory of God."* This scripture explains that everyone has come short of God's glory and needs redemption. Then Romans 6:23a states, *"For the wages of sin is death."* Here, we learn that the consequence of living a life of sin is death. Everyone will experience physical death as a result of the sin committed in the garden of Eden, but those who commit themselves to a life of sin will suffer eternal damnation in the lake of fire (Rev. 19).

Continue with the rest of verse 6:23 that says, *"but the gift of God is eternal life through Jesus Christ our Lord."* There is an alternative to suffering eternal damnation. We can accept the gift of salvation by accepting Jesus as our personal lord and savior. Then, Romans 5:8 says, *"But God commendeth his love toward us, in that, while we were yet sinners, Christ died for us."* We are able to receive the gift of salvation because Christ came to earth and shed His blood for us on the cross.

Continue to Romans 10: 9-10 which says, *"That if thou shalt confess with thy mouth the Lord Jesus, and shalt believe in thine heart that God hath raised him from the dead, thou shalt be saved.*

For with the heart man believeth unto righteousness; and with the mouth confession is made unto salvation." If we confess with our mouths that Jesus is the son of God, that he came and died for our sins, and that God raised Him from the dead, we will receive salvation.

Finish with Romans 10:13, which states, *"For whosoever shall call upon the name of the Lord shall be saved."* Call upon the name of God by saying these words, **"Lord Jesus, come into my heart and save me Lord. I believe that you are the Son of God who came and died on the cross for my sins. I believe that you rose from the grave. I also believe that you now sit in heaven on the right side of the Father, making intersession for me. I accept you as my Lord and my Savior."**

Now that you have confessed with your mouth that Jesus is the son of God and that He died for our sins and rose from the grave, **YOU ARE NOW SAVED!!!!** You will spend your eternity in heaven.

The next step is very important- you must find a bible-based church that teaches the word of God and confesses the Lord Jesus Christ to be the son of God. Don't delay. Do this immediately. Do not leave yourself open to the enemy. Get connected with the saints of the Most High God and keep yourself covered with the unspotted blood of the lamb.

Here is my prayer for you.

Father God,
I thank you for the opportunity to minister your word to the unsaved, the unchurched, and the uncommitted. Father God, I pray now for the souls who have just received the gift of salvation. Lord Father, they have opened their hearts to you, and I know that you have received them into your kingdom and written their names in the Book of Life. Father God, I pray that you will touch their

lives and show yourself mightily before them. Let their eyes be opened by the scales falling off, allowing them to see clearly.

Father God, I even pray for the backslider, those who have turned away from you after receiving the gift of salvation. You said in your word that you desire that none would perish. So Lord, I send your word to them right now praying that they would confess the iniquity in their heart, repent, and turn from their evil ways, so that they may receive a life of abundance. You said in your word in Matthew Chapter 14, that every knee shall bow before you and every tongue will confess that Jesus is Lord.

Father God, I pray now that we all come under subjection to your word and that we will humbly submit our lives to you. I ask all these things in the name of my Lord and Savior Jesus Christ. Amen, Amen, Amen!!!!

I will continue to pray for your success in your walk with God. Remember, this spiritual walk that you are about to embark on will not be an easy walk, but remember, the race is not given to the swift but to those who endure to the end.

Be blessed with heaven's best. I love you!

A Mother's Heart

About the Editor

Dr. Cassundra White-Elliott resides in California with her family, where as an English/Education professor she works for various community colleges and universities.

When writing, she writes with the direction of the Holy Spirit, in an effort to share with God's people all that He has for them.

In addition to teaching and writing, Dr. White-Elliott also serves as an evangelistic teacher. She is also the founder of International Women's Commission, a ministry that serves the needs of the entire person, by attending to healing the mind, body, soul, and spirit.

Dr. White-Elliott holds a Ph.D. in Education, a Master's in English Composition, and a Bachelor's in Education.

Dr. White-Elliott is also the founder of CLF Publishing, LLC. For your publishing needs, go online to www.clfpublishing.org.

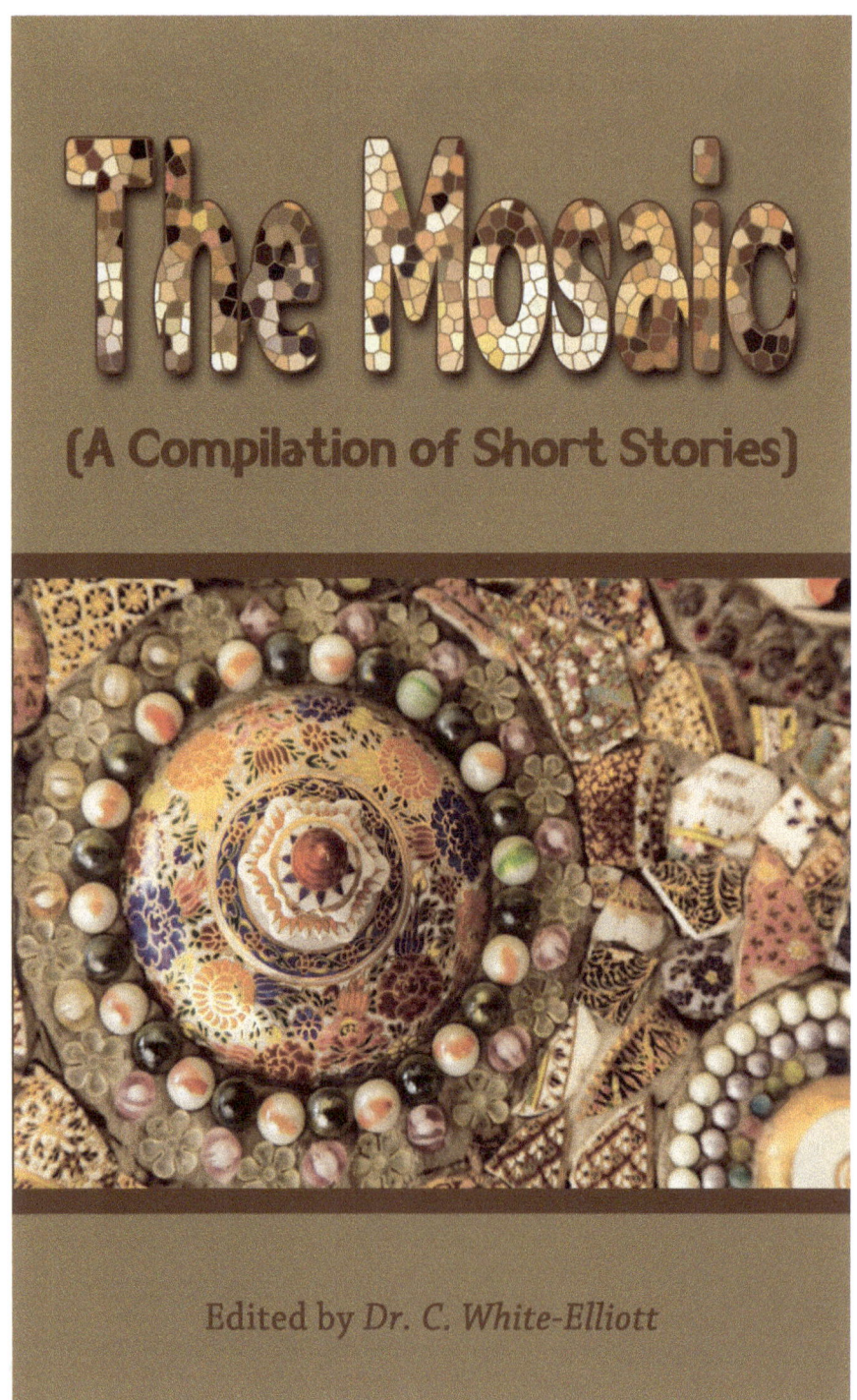

Dr. Cassundra White-Elliott

A Mother's Heart

www.ingramcontent.com/pod-product-compliance
Lightning Source LLC
Chambersburg PA
CBHW070539170426
43200CB00011B/2476